Economists Can Be
Bad for Your Health

ALSO BY GEORGE P. BROCKWAY

The End of Economic Man

Economists Can Be Bad for Your Health

Second Thoughts on the Dismal Science

George P. Brockway

W. W. Norton & Company

NEW YORK • LONDON

First Edition

The text of this book is composed in Avanta, with the display set in Bulmer.
Composition and manufacturing by the Haddon Craftsmen, Inc.

Library of Congress Cataloging-in-Publication Data
Brockway, George P.
Economists can be bad for your health: and other essays on the dismal
science/George P. Brockway.
p.   cm.
Includes index.
1. Economics.   I. Title.
HB171.B64985   1995
330—dc20   95-8269
ISBN 0-393-03884-X

W.W. Norton & Company, Inc., 500 Fifth Avenue, New York, N.Y. 10110
W.W. Norton & Company Ltd., 10 Coptic Street, London WC1A 1PU

1 2 3 4 5 6 7 8 9 0

All of the material in this book appeared originally, although on a few occasions in somewhat different form, under the rubric "The Dismal Science" in *The New Leader*.

for Myron Kolatch
editor and friend

Contents

———————

9

Economists Can Be
Bad for Your Health

Trust in Life

————————

I see by the papers that the New York State Education Department is preparing a new social studies curriculum that will include a year's course in economics in the twelfth grade. They didn't have anything like that when I was in high school; so my initial reaction to the news is that it can't be a very good idea. On second thought, I will allow that it might be all right if they ran the course my way (which they probably won't I reflect sourly). And that thought leads me to wonder how I'd go about it if I had my druthers.

I should perhaps say at the outset that I come by my sourness in the line of duty. I once had to edit a textbook on educational psychology, and it almost turned my brain to oatmeal, and mushy oatmeal, at that. Somewhat later I wasted several years trying to put together a series of secondary-school literature anthologies. I'd had some experience with college-level anthologies; but it developed that professional educators were unanimously of the opinion that what succeeded with eighteen-year-olds was quite different from what seventeen-year-olds could or should be interested in. I didn't believe it then, and I still don't. That there is a difference, I recognize. That it is as great as pretended by those who call themselves educationists, I

13

doubt. That it should be an objective of an educational program to narrow the difference, I contend.

A year after boys and girls are graduated from high school, they will become young men and women old enough to vote. Not old enough to drink (who is?), but old enough to vote and bear arms. About half of them will go to work at once — or try to. I'll not now embroil myself in the question of whether some familiarity with our literary heritage would make them better citizens leading better lives. However all that may be, it does seem altogether fitting that some effort should be made to teach them how the world of work works.

The trouble, of course, is that we grown-ups don't agree on how the world of work works. There is scant chance of satisfying both the Economic Policy Institute and the American Enterprise Institute. What pleases the AFL-CIO doesn't always please the Business Roundtable. It is happily no longer fashionable for us to call each other Communists (I was astonished to learn the other day that the John Birch Society still exists), but we nevertheless generate a good many British Thermal Units in charging each other with operating a front for special interests.

On the record, the schools are entitled to anticipate a lot of trouble when they start to teach economics. It will not be surprising if they try to avoid the problem by reducing the subject to the least common denominator of their students' capabilities and fancies. Such solutions are not unheard of. In the case of economics, the least common denominator is likely to be that of our grown-up prejudices, and the resulting pablum is liable to be not merely non-nourishing but positively poisonous. The world of work is not an uncomplicated and noncontroversial place, and it is dangerous for citizens to think that it is.

The first problem in any course is to discover what the subject is. As it happens, I can lay my hands on the first sentence of a book I've been writing, which goes like this: "Economics is the study of the principles whereby people exchange money for goods and services." Although I go on to say that "people" is the most important word in the definition, I think that with twelfth-graders I'd concentrate on another word: "money."

No one should object to talking about money in a course on economics, and that's what I'd talk about. Money is, in fact, an ideal subject to talk with kids about. It is something everyone deals with every day; it is something people talk about all the time; and it is something people have the most extraordinary ideas about. So talking about money is talking about something both familiar and full of surprises.

Money is, moreover, the absolutely essential idea in economics. If you try to teach economics without money, all the other subjects in the course fall away or disappear. What can you say about prices if you don't have the idea of money? Obviously nothing, because prices must be stated in terms of some monetary unit. Without money, what becomes of production or supply? It reduces to agriculture or engineering. Without money, what becomes of consumption or demand? It reduces to physiology and psychology. If you don't have money, you don't have economics. You have all these other disciplines, which are good in their own right, and which are often confused with economics, but which are not economics.

My first units (that's educationese for chapters) would be on what happens when you go to work. You do what the job requires for a day or a week or (if it's a classy job) a month, and then you get paid for what you've done. Nothing mysterious about that. But you have in effect lent your employer your earnings for the period. In the rare cases when you get paid in advance, your employer lends money to you. There is no way you can get paid instantaneously for the work you do each instant; so you and your employer have to trust each other.

Now, the interesting thing is that this mutual trust is creative. By working you have increased the goods in the economy, and by lending your employer your earnings you have increased the capital in the economy. This could not have happened unless your employer made the job possible; but if your employer had to pay you in advance, he or she would have less money to spend on machinery and materials.

There is a further role for trust. Not only do you and your employer have to trust each other, but you both have to have faith in the economy and in the nation that sponsors it. Your employer wouldn't hire you unless he or she was confident (*fides* = faith) that there was a market that would pay good money for what you together produce; and you wouldn't work unless you were confident the economy would let you enjoy the money you earn. The money you have has no worth except as you are able to credit it as worthy of your trust.

In the other direction, money is what makes it possible for you and your employer to agree. You will do so much work for so much money. Without money, your relationship would be at best sharecropping and at worst slavery.

The point of this first part of the course would be that money is faith, trust, credit. It is not paper or silver or gold. And the moral of this first part of the course might be stated by paraphrasing Baron Heyst of Joseph Conrad's *Victory*: Woe to the nation whose citizens have not learned to hope, to love—and to put their trust in life.

This moral would, I am afraid, be the hardest part of the course to get over; so I'd be prepared to spend a lot of time on it. I took my World War II basic training with a lot of kids from the Lower East Side of New York and from south Philadelphia (whites had been separated from blacks at the reception centers), and I was bewildered by the difficulty many of them had in even imagining the possibility of a disinterested action. They had what has since come to be called street smarts, and they suspected an angle to everything. Intellectuals, too, find trust a difficult idea, for intellectual smarts are a facility in uncovering unconscious motivations and special interests. And conservative smarts are a passion for gold that bespeaks a sentimental longing for something more trustworthy than the national economy and our fellow citizens.

So establishing the nature and need of trustworthiness would take time, especially since street, intellectual, and conservative smarts are sadly often right in clinging to their suspicions in specific situations. For the sake of the economy, and for the sake of the individuals who participate in it, however, it is more important to do right than to be right.

By this time, we're probably well into January or even February, and the next group of units would take some time, too. The subject now would be fractional reserve banking and how it works. This is comparatively simple, though I doubt that even two of the next twenty people you meet could explain it to you. And for lack of time, the last group would be on private debt and public debt, and how they're alike, and how they're unlike, and maybe even a hint or two about their connection with inflation and employment. This could well be highly controversial, but thank goodness the school year would be almost over.

Do you think it would be next to impossible to get these ideas over to seventeen-year-olds? I do, too. But I also think that if the next generation doesn't understand money any better than the present generation, it won't matter too much what else they learn about the economy. They'd be much better off reading those high-school anthologies I never published.

[10/84]

The Fear of Full Employment

The other day a friend sent me a clipping from the morning paper. My friend is a poet, whom I occasionally charge with deliberate obfuscation, and she was, she said, getting some of her own back. "What gives?" she asked, showing she can use ordinary speech when she wants to. "Who's obfuscating now?"

The clipping she sent me read as follows: "Economists have become more pessimistic in recent days because the most recent batch of economic statistics, including yesterday's strong employment report, suggests that the economy may be picking up steam and may overheat." This was, of course, a run-of-the-mill news note of the sort we have all read many times, and I wondered why it was bothering my friend. I gave her a ring. "Surely your *Webster* or *OED* has all the words," I remarked cuttingly, "and only a couple of them have more than three syllables."

"Yes," she replied, "and many of my poems are made up of even shorter words. What I'd like to know is, what kinds of idiots are made pessimistic by an economy's picking up steam? If it's in danger of overheating, why not put more water in the boiler? I know you economists are even more devoted to metaphors than we poets are, but I thought you were all enamored of the one about a rising tide lifting all boats."

"Don't look at me," I objected. "I'm not one of 'you economists.' The pessimists of your clipping know that if business gets really good the Federal Reserve Board will get nervous about inflation and raise the interest rate, and that lowers the capitalized value of all stocks and bonds."

"You mean, if I invest my royalties in a hundred-dollar bond that pays five dollars a year, and if the interest rate goes up to 10 percent, then my bond will be worth only fifty dollars?"

"I don't know how a poet gets a hundred dollars in royalties," I said, "but you're absolutely right."

"Eureka!" she cried. "I've outdone Archimedes! There's no way the stock market can go up."

"Keep your shirt on," I advised.

But she paid no attention. "If business is bad," she said, "poor earnings will send stock prices down. And if business is good, higher interest rates will send the market down. Why hasn't anyone discovered this before? If you sell short, you can't lose. Please give me the name of a good discount broker. I sincerely want to be rich."

It's a shame that my friend is merely one of the unacknowledged legislators of the world. We could use some of her guileful questioning in high places, and particularly in regard to the received doctrine that high employment makes for high inflation. Practically all economists, businessmen, bankers, politicians, and journalists are united in endorsement of this doctrine. Their unanimity is very curious—first, because few, if any, other economics propositions command such universal assent; second, because it is among the most unequivocally dismal notions in all this dismal science; and third, because there is no evidence whatever to support it. I don't mean that no evidence is offered; I mean that the evidence offered is false or irrelevant or both.

If the proposition weren't so dismal, it wouldn't be worth troubling about. But look at what it means: It assumes that inflation is the worst economic misfortune that could befall us, and it asserts that in order to avoid—or simply to control—inflation, we must prevent several million people from having jobs. Even if all these millions were fully qualified and fully motivated, given the inexorable working of the system, they would still be unemployable.

Let's think about that for a minute. It is the practically unanimous opinion of everyone who talks about the subject that our system, of which we are told to be so proud, must condemn upwards of seven million people to lives of undeserved squalor, uselessness, and hopelessness. Of course, that adds up to fifteen or twenty million men, women, and children when you count their dependents.

If I believed that our system were inevitably, necessarily, and indeed systematically that cruel, I'd be on the barricades in a minute—and I like to think I would be joined by you and by most of those who thoughtlessly repeat the dismal doctrine. My God, they're talking about fellow human beings!

I don't believe our system has to be that cruel. It is that cruel, but it doesn't have to be. We're given to understand that right now, with inflation running at about 3.5 percent and unemployment at about 6.5 percent, things are perhaps actually a little better than can be expected. Certainly our leaders consider them so good that they seem able to congratulate themselves without embarrassment.

Well, consulting *Economic Report of the President, 1994,* I find that since World War II there have been thirty-four years in which unemployment was at a lower rate, twenty-one years with lower inflation, and no fewer than twenty years where both inflation and unemployment were lower. Not only that, but in the year of lowest unemployment, inflation was lower than in all except four of the forty-odd years in question. In the year of highest inflation, unemployment was higher than in seven of the years. These figures certainly do not support the doctrine.

That may be said to be the small picture. A bigger picture is presented by the runaway inflations of our time that are regularly flashed on the screen to scare us into doing something drastic about inflation now, before we all have to get wheelbarrows to carry our worthless money to market to buy a loaf of black bread.

Besides the Weimar Republic runaway, the prime examples are Hungary after World War II and Brazil recently. If the doctrine were sound, those countries would have had full employment and overheated economies to start their runaways. Exactly the contrary, though, was the case. Each one suffered from appalling unemployment, and Brazil still does, without in any way impeding or controlling the inflation. These examples do not support the doctrine, either.

To complete the empirical record, we may note that today, of all industrialized nations, Japan has the second lowest unemployment and the lowest inflation.

In short, there is no relevant evidence reliably connecting high inflation and full employment. We have not, after all, ever had full employment except in wartime, when inflation of civilian prices is to be expected because civilian production is necessarily curtailed. On the other hand, we have many times had inflation in peacetime, and we have perversely tried to control it by raising the interest rate in order to *curtail* production.

My poet friend asked me why, if the unemployed had jobs, they couldn't produce goods at least equal in value to their wages. I couldn't think why. "Then there wouldn't be more money chasing fewer goods, would there?" she asked. "So why isn't full employment the *cure* for inflation?"

Well, why isn't it?

[10/88]

The Productivity Scam

A couple of Sundays ago the *New York Times* business section had one of its recurring roundups of professional opinion on productivity. This is a live issue because publicists and politicians keep it alive. At least two presidential commissions are supposed to have been working on the question for the past decade or so (though no one knows the results, if any). Innumerable editorials have been written on it, and not a few books.

Yet the whole thing is an elaborate scam, because what is presented as a value-free study by sober social scientists is actually a struggle over the distribution of the national income. Some (perhaps most) of those perpetrating the scam may know not what they do. It is a scam, nevertheless.

As pseudo-science, the argument goes like this: Of the various factors of production, labor is the largest. Employees' compensation—wages, salaries, bonuses, fringe benefits—comes to about three-fifths of the gross national product. This being so, it would seem plausible to take this largest factor as an index of the efficiency of the whole.

As the *Times* put it, "A worker who produces 100 widgets an hour, for example, is clearly more productive than a worker who produces only 50 widgets an hour." There are many sleepers in this seemingly innocent example, and the *Times* is aware of some of them: "the machines that are used, the worker's education or skill, advances in technology, the working environment." The worker can be praised or blamed for few of the items in this little list. Most of them are someone else's doing. This fact is not noticed by the judgmental types who complain that people don't work as hard as they used to.

But the trouble with the productivity index goes back further than that. The trouble starts with the GNP itself. The GNP hasn't got to do with widgets at all, or with shoes or ships or sealing wax. The reason for this is obvious enough: You can't add shoes and ships and sealing wax to widgets any more than you can add apples and pears. All you can add are the prices of the widgets and shoes and so on, and you get a result in dollars that depends as much on the prices of widgets and shoes as on the numbers of widgets and shoes.

This is true for the economy as a whole, and it is also true for the firms that make it up. Even that rare company that makes widgets and only widgets judges its productivity in numbers of dollars rather than numbers of widgets. If it manufactures a hundred widgets but can sell only fifty, the remaining fifty are not products but waste. Other companies, which deal in a variety of products, have no choice but to measure their total output in dollars.

Nor is this procedure necessary only in market economies. In the purest communism of our time (the brief reign of the Gang of Four in China), several streets in Shanghai were lined with thousands of boilers quietly rusting under the plane trees. Somebody had built them and no doubt got a commendation for exceeding his quota, but there was no use for them. They were not products but waste, and (if they're not still there) they had eventually to be broken up for scrap.

The next trouble with the GNP comes with what it includes and what it excludes. The *Times* article provides a good example of the mischief that results. "Increased regulation," says the *Times*, "aimed at such things as clean air and water and increased safety in the workplace, . . . absorbed management time and business resources in the 70's. Now that the pace of new regulation has slowed, if not reversed, business will be freer to concentrate its money and effort on other things, such as productivity."

You've heard so much of this kind of talk that you may not be immediately struck by how fatuous it is. But if you will read the passage again, you will notice the unstated (and unstatable) assumption that clean air and water and increased safety are nothing in comparison with more widgets or cheaper widgets or anything at all (a widget being the ultimate nondescript object). Now, there may be some things more important than clean air, but a widget isn't one of them. In a rational world, what you produce is a more important question than productivity.

Productivity is a ratio, a common fraction. So far we have dealt only with the numerator. The denominator is suspect in its own way. The figure usually used is the total hours worked by everyone in producing the GNP. This is a moldy fudge. Since you can't think how to quantify (except in dollars, of which more later) the relative contributions of the designer of the widget, the operator of the machine that stamps it out, and the fellow who sweeps up the scraps, you sweep the problem out with the scraps and conclude that Gertrude Stein would have been right if she had said, "Hour is an hour is an hour." Or as Karl Marx did put it, "We save ourselves a superfluous operation, and simplify our analysis, by the assumption, that the labour of the workman employed by the capitalist is unskilled average labour."

On this basis, you'd have to say that if a skilled journeyman carpenter could increase his output 50 percent by taking on an unskilled apprentice, the result would be a 25 percent decrease in his productivity. You'd also have to say that the apprentice's productivity was equal to the journeyman's. Worse than this, you'd have to say—and people do say—that it's better for national productivity to have millions of men and women unemployed than for them to be working but producing less than their co-workers. Thus, the *Times* says, "The entry of 20 million new and inexperienced workers into the labor force during the 1970's acted as a drag on productivity."

Any theory that makes you say things like that is silly, and any figures that lead to such conclusions are mischievous. Productivity, at least as everyone measures it, is a grievously misleading notion. If you take it seriously, you believe that clean air and water and increased safety are bad and should be opposed. And if you take it seriously, you believe that employing young people and women and blacks and others without experience is also bad, and that therefore an unemployment rate of 7 or 8 percent is not only acceptable but desirable.

It may occur to you to wonder why the denominator of the productivity ratio is "hours worked." Why not "workers' compensation"? Then at least you'd not have silly results like our journeyman/apprentice example or the all-too-real unemployment problem. Then you wouldn't have to pretend, as the *Times* does, that management has been wasting its valuable time on the environment.

You would, however, be in danger of calling attention to one of the hidden aspects of the scam, and that is the place of management—especially top management—in all this. For the CEO is a wage slave just like the operator of the widget machine. As long as you talk about hours worked, you meld his allegedly productive hours with the less valuable hours of the operator, thus improving the index and demonstrating your scientific willingness to put the faltering American workingman in as favorable a light as possible.

And you also diminish the chance that someone might point out that some CEOs are paid five or six *thousand* times as much as widget operators. And someone might put together some figures separating management productivity from working-stiff productivity, and you'd have a whole new ball game. It would no longer seem that the Japanese are catching up with us because their production workers are workaholics while ours are goofoffs; the catching up, if any, would then appear to be due to the fact that they have fewer managers, who have fewer Learjets, stretch limousines, three-martini lunches, tax shelters, and golden parachutes.

The scam has still another aspect. Labor may be the largest but it is not the only factor of production. Looking back on what the *Times* said about other factors ("the machines that are used, the worker's education or skill, advances in technology, the working environment"), you will note that the first and last of these are supplied by capital, while the second is largely the responsibility of the state, and the third is a joint responsibility of capital and the state. On this basis, a capital productivity index would be at least as reasonable as a labor productivity index. (I have prepared such an index, and it moves in the opposite direction to the labor index.)

And you can carry this a step further. For though productive capital is not money, it is bought with money and money has a cost, which is interest. The prime rate has gone from 1.5 percent (really and truly) in 1947 to 12.5 percent today (1984), having had flings as high as 21.5 percent in the meantime. In other words, every dollar American industry now pays (actually, or as opportunity cost) for interest is able to buy only one-eighth as much of capital goods as it could have at the end of the war (and this is without counting inflation).

This is the real drag on the American economy, and on the world economy, too. As I said at the beginning, the uproar about labor productivity is a scam to distract attention from a massive shift in the distribution of the goods of the economy. The share of nonmanagerial labor is being reduced; the share of managerial labor is being increased; and the share of those who do not labor, but merely have money, is being increased most of all.

[5/84]

Are You Naturally Unemployed?

Currently the hottest ticket on the economics market is the doctrine of the natural rate of unemployment. The implications of the doctrine are such that they don't, as the saying goes, bear thinking about. Nevertheless, I propose to try to think about them here and now.

The expression "the natural rate of unemployment" was apparently coined by Milton Friedman in his presidential address to the American Economic Association on December 29, 1967. Friedman was clear that what he called the natural rate was not a natural law (like, say, $s=\frac{1}{2}gt^2$). "On the contrary," he said, "many of the market characteristics that determine its level [such as minimum-wage laws] are man-made and policy-made." Yet he saw and, I believe, still sees something inexorable in the idea.

Friedman said he used the word "natural" because the idea was comparable to "the natural rate of interest," a notion advanced by the Swedish economist Knut Wicksell in 1898. Wicksell is worth reading (though perhaps not on this issue), but for the moment we need note only that he is thought by many to have anticipated Keynes in some ways. And as to Keynes, we need remember particularly that his initial quarrel with the clas-

sic economists was that they believed involuntary unemployment was impossible. Since whatever is "natural" is *ipso facto*
involuntary, Friedman, too, broke with the classics on this point.
I hasten to insist that Friedman is not now and never has been a
Keynesian or a neo-Keynesian, and certainly not a Post Keynesian.

The natural rate of unemployment is thus an idea that reso-
nated unexpectedly in many corners of modern economic
thought. In its pure form it goes like this: Given the civil laws,
customs, and institutions of the economy (though Friedman is
not now and never has been an institutionalist follower of Thor-
stein Veblen or John R. Commons), beyond a certain point any
increase in the rate of unemployment will result in deflation and
a recession that will continue until wages fall to a level to encourage entrepreneurs to start hiring again; on the other hand,
any decrease in unemployment will result in inflation and a recession that will continue until employment returns to its natural rate.

The idea was not immediately embraced by the profession.
Very likely, thin-skinned economists were timid about saying
that joblessness could be your patriotic duty. This difficulty was
overcome when somebody (I'm sorry I don't know who) came
up with a name that obscures the implications of the idea and
has, moreover, an acronym that soothingly sounds like the name
of a languorous South Sea isle. The new name is "nonaccelerat-
ing inflationary rate of unemployment," or NAIRU.

The NAIRU was 3 or 4 percent at the end of World War II. It
reached 5 or 6 percent in 1975, after the Federal Reserve Board
raised interest rates in its quixotic response to the first OPEC
embargo. And it appears to be around 6 percent today (the current rate of unemployment is dismal from any point of view).

Let us be sure we understand what a NAIRU of 6 percent
means. It means that, given our present labor force of some 127
million men and women, about 7.6 million of them must be
unemployed *through no fault of their own*. Forgive me for raising
my voice, but we must see clearly that NAIRU won't work if

unemployment is the result of stupidity, poor training, laziness, lawlessness, or unreasonably high wage demands—if unemployment is, as the classical economists said, voluntary. The NAIRU people are not the people of Reaganesque anecdotes (if such people there ever were) who flit from job to unemployment insurance to job as the spirit moves them. Stupid, incompetent, lazy, lawless, or grasping people do not compete for existing jobs; it is the function of NAIRU people to make holders of existing jobs fear for their positions and so acquiesce in low pay, unsafe or Quayle-approved working conditions, frayed fringe benefits, and non-union shops.

Perhaps you will now sense another resonance of the natural rate of unemployment. It is the stern, impassioned tread of Karl Marx's industrial reserve army. "The industrial reserve army," Marx wrote, "during periods of stagnation and average prosperity, weighs down the active labor-army; during periods of over-production and paroxysm, it holds its pretensions in check." Friedman might have put it somewhat more gracefully.

How did the soldiers of the industrial reserve army get recruited? They weren't rounded up by press gangs like those that helped Britannia rule the waves, but their fate has not been dissimilar. They did not volunteer, and they were not drafted; they were in the wrong place at the wrong time, and many of them were simply born wrong, just as Rockefellers and such happened to be born right. They are victims of crashingly bad luck.

From time to time, demographers publish studies averring that only a percentage (say 10 percent or 5 percent or perhaps 1 percent) are what we used to call lifers and spend their entire lives in the industrial reserve army, or that only some other percentage (say 12 percent) serve more than twenty-seven weeks at a time, while Horatio Alger and his like are discharged in a matter of days. We may accept these studies, or most of them, at their face value and still observe that those in the industrial reserve army serve as a consequence of crashingly bad luck, and that they serve in our interest and indeed in our stead. This being the case, it cannot be denied that our economic system—a system said to depend on the natural rate of unemployment—would self-destruct if it were not fundamentally unjust. It is clever to say that life is unfair; it is corrupt to raise unfairness to a principle of control.

Joseph Schumpeter celebrated capitalism as "the civilization of inequality and the family fortune." I cannot do that. I cannot understand doing that. I cannot settle for NAIRU in any of its forms. I can accept the military draft and have in fact been drafted. It is possible in time of war to show citizens, chosen by lot, their duty to risk their lives in defense of the nation that nurtured them. It is not possible to show anyone a duty to lead a life of squalor and despair in order that others may be free to choose among moderately priced commodities.

If there really is a natural rate of unemployment for our system, the system is immoral. If it is immoral, we should change it. Some will say that even with NAIRU, ours is the best system seen so far, and others will say that NAIRU applies to all systems. Despite these answers, improvements are possible.

To share the burden of NAIRU fairly, we might take Marx's metaphor literally and institute a legitimate draft for the industrial reserve army. It is unlikely that there would be volunteers, and there should be no exemptions of any kind (except for the unemployable). Membership in the army probably would be by nuclear families, unless children were put out for adoption while their parents served. There would no doubt be problems with the definition of a family, but I'm sure that, given goodwill, solutions could be found.

Every able-bodied family in the nation would pull at least one hitch in the army. Service would consist of living without personal assets or income (including imputed income, as for example, decent food, clothing, and shelter) for a period. I imagine two or three years would suffice at the present natural rate of unemployment. For ease of administration, it might be convenient in some cases for families to exchange homes. Certainly the houses of wealthy draftees could not be left vacant without inflating the general cost of housing.

Private charity also would have to be rigorously controlled to prevent favoritism and corruption. Food stamps, Aid to Families with Dependent Children, Medicaid, and the like (including workfare if finally enacted) would be available. Of course, for the army to serve its purpose, recruits must be able to work, but their availability would have to be in accordance with length of service. It wouldn't be fair for me to be enlisted one day and hired by a friend the next.

Perhaps all that strikes you as preposterous. It certainly seems preposterous to me. But the whole idea of placidly accepting a natural rate of unemployment strikes me as far more preposterous.

Now, looking back at the theory of NAIRU, we note that the general price level is to be controlled by holding down only one of the factors of production (labor). Why shouldn't we also hold down the rate of interest? Since inflation of the costs of production is the issue, why shouldn't we have NAIRI as well as NAIRU?

"But," cry the governors of the Federal Reserve Board, "we control inflation by raising the interest rate." They know not what they do. In the forty years since 1951, when the Reserve freed itself from its wartime agreement with the Treasury to hold rates down, the percentage of GNP that goes to pay interest on debt of the nonfinancial sector has gone from 4.59 percent to 20.51 percent. Let me put it another way: In 1951 the interest bill of American corporations was about one-twelfth of their wage bill, whereas today it is more than a third. If the 1951 ratio still applied, today's costs would be roughly $845 billion less than they actually are, and the price level would be lower by a considerably greater amount.

By raising the interest rate (even now it is more than double what it was in 1951), the Federal Reserve Board has contributed to (if not mainly caused) inflation. It has then restrained the inflation it caused by bringing on recession, which keeps the industrial reserve army in being.

So not only does NAIRU serve reactionary interests in keeping wages in check; it is a convenient reactionary ploy in other situations. Public works cannot be used to reinvigorate the economy because the increase in employment would violate NAIRU. Likewise, although doctrinaire free traders may admit that selective protection might protect or restore as many as two million jobs, NAIRU forbids it. And so on.

In short, the nasty theory of a natural rate of unemployment is counterproductive as well as immoral.

[8/92]

Bankers Have the Classic COLA

In "The Fear of Full Employment" we examined some of the fallacies behind the almost universally held doctrine that full employment makes for high inflation. This time we'll look at another almost universally held doctrine, namely, that raising the interest rate is the cure for whatever inflation exists. An astonishing thing about the latter doctrine is that no one bothers to say why it should work. The *New York Times,* which never mentions the prime interest rate without pedantically explaining what it is, regularly reports without question that if the Consumer Price Index starts to rise, the Federal Reserve Board will have to raise the interest rate.

Economists divide what they call the nominal or "money" interest rate (which is what you pay) into two parts: "real" interest (what they think you'd pay if the economy were stable) and an allowance for inflation. The allowance for inflation is what in other sectors of the economy is called a cost-of-living adjustment, or COLA. People with money to spare are said to be enticed into lending by the prospect of getting back their money at a stated time with stated interest. What they want back is not the money, but the money's purchasing power; and in inflationary times the only way to get back the same purchasing power is to get back more money. Hence the Bankers' COLA.

Of course, bankers don't call it a COLA. They have, in fact, been unremitting in propagandizing the notion that COLAs are bad and greedy and inflationary and likely to cause the downfall of the Republic. The COLAs bankers talk about are those that appear (or used to) in labor contracts, where they are manifestly an increased cost of doing business for companies with such contracts, and those that appear in Social Security and other pension payments, where they are manifestly an increased cost of running the government. (Another COLA, seldom mentioned, is the partial indexing of the income tax.) Since increased costs of doing business increase prices, and increased costs of running the government increase taxes (or the deficit), it is argued, with reason, that COLAs are inflationary.

The propaganda against them (coupled with high unemployment and underemployment) has pretty well knocked cost-of-living clauses out of labor contracts. The Social Security COLAs are somewhat more secure because there are more worried senior citizens than alert union members. Even so, the steady cacophony from investment bankers (when they take time off from promoting leveraged buyouts, which they evidently don't think inflationary) has put the American Association of Retired Persons on the defensive. The Bankers' COLA, however, is accepted as a natural law and discussed matter-of-factly in the textbooks, while the others are deplored as the work of greedy special interests out to line their own pockets at the expense of the nation and its God-fearing citizens.

One way of stating the Bankers' COLA is that it is the difference between the interest rate now and that of some earlier, less inflationary time. The prime rate in December 1988, when this was written, was 10.5 percent. The rate is scandalously volatile and has been both higher and lower since then. Other figures quoted below are also dated. The rate of the Bankers' COLA will therefore vary with the date selected, but the argument of the COLA's effects nevertheless stands.

In the forty-odd years since the end of World War II, there is one stretch, from 1959 through 1965, when the CPI and the prime were both substantially stable. In those seven years the CPI varied from 0.8 percent to 1.7 percent, and the prime from 4.48 percent to 4.82 percent. (Readers with a political turn of mind will note that the presidents in this period were a Republican and two Democrats—Dwight D. Eisenhower, John F. Kennedy, and Lyndon B. Johnson.) The Bankers' COLA was evidently no more than 1.7 percent in those years, and the "real" interest rate was somewhere between 3.5 percent and 4.5 percent.

Let's accept the higher figure, even though it is substantially higher than, for example, the rate in the years when the foundations of the modern economy were laid. Subtracting 4.5 percent "real" interest from the current prime, we determine that the current Bankers' COLA is, conservatively, 6 percent.

But only about a tenth of outstanding loans were written in the past year, and many go back twenty-five or thirty years. Over the past ten years the CPI has increased an average of 6.01 percent a year. That is remarkably (and coincidentally) close to our estimate of the current Bankers' COLA. The average gets higher as we go back fifteen and twenty years, and falls slightly if we go back twenty-five years. Consequently, if the Bankers' COLA has been doing what it's supposed to do, we are not overstating the case in saying that today it is running at about 6 percent.

Now, the present (1988) outstanding debt of domestic nonfinancial sectors is about $8,300 billion. This figure includes everything from the federal debt to the charge you got hit with when you didn't pay your bank's credit card on time; excluded are the debts banks owe each other and, for some reason, charges on your nonbank credit card. The cost of the Bankers' COLA for this year therefore comes to about $498 billion (6 percent of $8,300 billion).

As the late Senator Everett McKinley Dirksen would have

said, we're talking about real money. Let's try to put it in perspective. At the moment the CPI is said to be about 4.5 percent (less, you will have noticed, than the Bankers' COLA, because bankers expect inflation to get worse). Since the GNP is currently about $4,500 billion, inflation is currently costing us 4.5 percent of that, or $202.5 billion. The Bankers' COLA is thus costing us almost two and a half times as much as the inflation it is claimed to offset.

So we come to Brockway's Law No. 1: Given the fact that outstanding indebtedness is greater than GNP (as is always the case, in good years and bad), the Bankers' COLA costs more than the total cost of inflation, at whatever rate.

Another comparison: The Bankers' COLA costs close to three times as much as the federal deficit the bankers moan about. (If there were no Bankers' COLA, we'd be running a surplus, not a deficit.)

Also: The Bankers' COLA costs many times more than all the other COLAs put together and about fifty times—repeat, fifty times—more than the Social Security COLA that so exercises investment bankers. (If there were no Bankers' COLA, none of the other COLAs would exist, because the cost of living would not be going up.)

Also: The Bankers' COLA costs more than giving every working man and woman in the land, from part-time office boy to CEO, a 10 percent raise. (So much for the fear of full employment.)

Since the Bankers' COLA costs the economy more than inflation does, without it there would in effect be no inflation. Other things being equal, there would actually be deflation. And of course very great changes would follow if so large a factor as the Bankers' COLA were eliminated. Reducing the interest rate to its "real" level would quickly and powerfully stimulate investment in productive enterprise, with a consequent growth in employment. It would trigger a one-time surge in the stock and bond markets, followed by a gradual tapering off of speculation.

As matters stand now, the Bankers' COLA is an incubus of terrible weight depressing the economy. That this is so is revealed by the statistics whose subject is people rather than things. The standard of living of the median family is falling, even with two earners per family much more common than formerly. The number of people living in poverty is growing, and within that group the number of those who work full time yet are poverty stricken is growing still faster. The rate of unemployment—even counting part-timers as fully employed, and not counting at all those too discouraged to keep looking for work—would have been shocking a few years ago. These are signs of recession, of bad times.

The interest cost is the only one that has a general effect on the economy. We used to hear a lot about the wage-price spiral, but a wage increase in the automobile industry (for many years the pundits' whipping boy) works its way through the economy slowly and uncertainly. Initially it affects only the price of automobiles, and it never brings about a uniform wage scale. Wages of grocery clerks remain low, and all wages in Mississippi remain low. A boost in the prime rate of a prominent bank, on the other hand, immediately affects the rates charged by every bank in the country; and while it is possible for borrowers to shop around a bit for a loan, they find that rates vary within a very narrow range.

More important, interest costs affect all prices, because all businesses must have money, even if they don't have to borrow it, and the cost of money is interest.

Vastly more important, the Bankers' COLA is a forecast, a prediction, a prophecy. The figures we have been working with are from the past, but bankers—including, especially, those who make up the Federal Reserve Board—set rates that will have to be paid decades into the future. Well into the twenty-first century, for instance, we will be paying up to 15.75 percent interest on a trillion dollars' worth of Treasury bonds sold in the wonder-working days of former Federal Reserve Chairman Paul A. Volcker.

So we come to Brockway's Law No. 2: Raising the interest rate doesn't cure inflation; it causes it.

[1/89]

Life, Liberty, and Property

Ten score and seventeen years ago (give or take a few) Thomas Jefferson undertook, with minor assistance from John Adams, Benjamin Franklin, and others, to write the Declaration of Independence. Aside from the catalog of complaints against George III, there is one phrase or word of the Declaration that is of special economic significance. Or rather, like Sherlock Holmes's dog that didn't bark, there is one phrase or word that curiously isn't there. That word is "property."

We learned in school that Jefferson (perhaps unconsciously) picked up the phrase "life, liberty, and property" from John Locke, the philosopher of the Glorious Revolution, and changed the last item in the series. In the first edition of Morison and Commager's textbook (the one I studied), we read that "Jefferson substituted for the term 'property' the word 'happiness': a characteristic and illuminating stroke on the part of this social philosopher who throughout his life placed human rights first."

Actually, Locke didn't use the precise words thus attributed to him. In his so-called *Second Treatise of Government*, several similar phrases occur: "life, health, liberty, or possessions" (sec. 6), "lives, liberties, or estates, which I call by the general name, property" (sec. 123), and "life, liberty, or possession" (sec. 135).

The passage that is generally cited as a source for the Declaration reads: "Man . . . hath by nature a power . . . to preserve his property, that is, his life, liberty, and estate . . ." (sec. 87).

Historians have also noted that as Jefferson sat down to write the Declaration, George Mason handed him a copy of his preamble to the bill of rights proposed for the new Virginia constitution. In that preamble Mason described "inherent rights" as "the enjoyment of life and liberty, with the means of acquiring and possessing property, and pursuing and obtaining happiness and safety."

The change from "property" or "estate" to "pursuit of happiness" has aroused much comment. Dumas Malone was at pains to note that Jefferson was no Communist, and he doubted that there was "any significance in his omission of the word 'property' . . . and his substitution for it of the phrase 'pursuit of happiness.' " Page Smith thought the change largely rhetorical but called attention to Jefferson's reading of the Scottish philosopher James Harrington. Merrill D. Peterson felt that "Jefferson did not intend to depreciate the right of property when he omitted it from the Declaration, but considering it an instrumental value, as a means to human happiness, and recognizing its civil character, he could not elevate property to the status of an inalienable right."

There may be truth in all these speculations, though there is no hard evidence for any of them. In any case, there is a simpler and more conclusive explanation, which, as I now believe, was first suggested by Garry Wills (though I claim independent discovery). It is this: The Declaration lists the pursuit of happiness as an *inalienable* (or "unalienable") right. But property is an *alienable* right: You can buy it or sell it or give it away, and the state has a superior right of eminent domain. Thomas Jefferson was a more precise thinker than John Locke and a more subtle draftsman than George Mason.

That property be alienable was, in fact, a special concern of Jefferson's. He was especially proud of his role in abolishing entail and primogeniture, and was especially troubled by his legal

inability to free slaves, some of whom may have been his children, if you accept Fawn Brodie's account (Malone, Peterson,
and Wills do not; Smith and I do).

There is not, so far as I know, any indication in Jefferson—or
in Locke, Harrington, or Mason—of a view of property as other
than tangible. A thing or things may convey power, and for this
reason Harrington thought property ought to be widely (though
perhaps not universally) spread throughout the body politic. Jefferson is understood to have hoped for a nation of independent
farmers, and he in fact proposed that the Virginia constitution
give fifty acres of the public domain (Virginia's original grant ran
"from sea to sea") to landless citizens. Locke's position was
slightly different: "The preservation of property being the end of
government," he wrote, "and that for which men enter into society, it necessarily supposes and requires that the people should
have property." For all these men property could be taxed, divided, and alienated, but it remained something you could walk
on or touch or hold in your hand.

We continue to talk about property in much the same terms,
but today our property is more a bundle of rights than a bundle
of things. Those of a literary turn of mind will most easily see
what is meant by considering a literary property, which is only
incidentally a particular manuscript but is effectively a copy-
right, or a right to copy. The right to copy is itself a bundle of
rights: U.S. and Canadian book rights may be licensed to one
publisher, British rights to another, paperback rights to still others, while book club, first serial, second serial, translation, TV,
and movie rights may be sold, all separately. And so on, for what
may indeed be a bundle.

Even real estate is a bundle of rights, which is considerably
smaller than it was in Jefferson's time. Zoning laws, and now en-
vironmental laws, restrict the right to do as one pleases with
one's property. On the other side, some jurisdictions accept the
gift of improvement rights, reducing taxes accordingly, so that
one won't be tempted to sell natural beauty for real estate "development." Condominiums and cooperatives are different sorts

of bundles. In the city, air rights are bought and sold; in Texas, drilling or mineral or grazing rights may be detached from the bundle.

In the corporate world, property has become progressively attenuated. *The Modern Corporation and Private Property*, published by A. A. Berle and G. C. Means in 1933, documented the separation of management and control of a company from ownership, or the right to alienate it. The idea was in the air: *The Acquisitive Society*, a soporifically earnest little book by R. H. Tawney, had made a similar point in 1921. When the modern limited liability stock company was first formed in the nineteenth century, the owners were also managers. Today the stock certificate, which is evidence of "ownership," is, for all intents and purposes, merely a counter used in playing the market. Like the Cheshire cat, even the counter vanishes into thin air when options, index futures, and puts and calls are traded.

It may be added that the company property that is "owned" is no longer so tangible as it used to be. The tangible property of a company is important to the owners only if the company is liquidated, and even then they are likely to watch helplessly as the creditors make off with everything they can lay their hands on. A company's stock is worth something only so long as the company is a going concern, and then it is the price/earnings ratio that matters, not the tangible assets.

The liquification of property raises questions of its legitimacy. Locke held that "[a]s much land as a man tills, plants, improves, cultivates, and can use the product of, so much is his property." He felt that a man's possessions were limited to what he could use before they spoiled; he argued, however, that money was a store of value that allowed one to store as much as one wanted so long as society wasn't hurt. Since it has happened from time to time that great wealth is adverse to the interests of society, one wonders what to do about it. One wonders, too, what becomes of the legitimacy of property when the owners hold it pursuant to inheritance or speculation, rather than (as Locke theorized) as the result of their labors.

The remittance man has always bothered moralists like me. Tawney complained that every penny the "functionless investor" received was *ipso facto* a penny not available to those who did the work. Keynes, too, depreciated the role of the functionless investor. "Interest to-day," he wrote, "rewards no genuine sacrifice, any more than does the rent of land. . . . I see, therefore, the rentier aspect of capitalism as a transitional phase which will disappear when it has done its work."

As the world has turned, however, we have been trending in the opposite direction. Since the days of Arthur Burns, the Federal Reserve Board has agreed with the bankers that the thing to do with the interest rate is to raise it. This is great for functionless investors, but has brought grief for everybody else.

This trend will not be controlled, let alone reversed, until our economists and lawyers and statesmen can be persuaded that the issues confronting us are not technical but are, as Jefferson and his colleagues understood, deeply moral, and that what is moral today is different from what was moral at the time of the Declaration.

[7/83]

Who Killed the Savings and Loans?

_____

The way we're going, we're not getting close to the truth about what happened to the savings and loans. It's much easier to be bemused by the amount of money lost in the disaster, to be shocked by the skulduggery involved, to be flabbergasted by the bad judgment of rich men, to be titillated by political charge and countercharge.

The $500-billion fiasco has been a long time in preparation. The first official action leading up to it was taken as early as March 1951, when the Federal Reserve Board got the Treasury to agree to a slight advance in interest rates. In his _Memoirs_, President Harry S. Truman criticizes the Reserve for failing to live up to its part of the agreement; but as William Greider points out in _Secrets of the Temple_, the issue became moot with President Dwight D. Eisenhower's election. Wall Street won out over Washington. The Reserve has, ever since, been undisturbed in following its gleam.

When the media go beyond personalities, they explain that the S&Ls failed because they borrowed short and lent long. That is, they accepted deposits that could be withdrawn at will (thirty days' notice was often reserved but seldom enforced), and they lent against mortgages running thirty years into the future.

The curious fact, however, is that the S&Ls were deliberately set up to act in this way from their beginnings in the Great Depression. They were designed to perform two functions: First, they would offer a safe depository for the small savings of the middle class; second, they would aggregate those savings and lend them to finance middle-class home ownership. Because the functions were restricted, it was understood that expenses would likewise be restricted. S&Ls, it was reasoned, could therefore offer a little bit more than the going rate on the deposits and charge a little bit less than the going rate on the mortgages. And so it was.

The new S&Ls were successful for more than thirty years. They were substantially responsible for the United States' achieving the highest rate of home ownership in the world (a rate considerably higher than the present one). They were also substantially responsible for a rebirth of personal savings following the Depression. My wife and I were able to buy a home and start saving at a far younger age than either our parents or our children.

For all those years that they were contributing to the wealth and happiness of the American people, the S&Ls were borrowing short and lending long. Obviously, something else caused the downfall.

Plenty of people are ready to tell you the problem was inflation. Inflation is always bad for lenders. If the price level is rising at a rate of 5 percent a year, anyone lending $100 today will receive back only $95 in purchasing power a year from now. At the same time, naturally, inflation is good for borrowers, who borrow $100 today and pay back $95 in purchasing power next year.

But look at the performance of the S&Ls over the long run—specifically, over the life of a mortgage. In that run of twenty or thirty years a go-getting middle-class American will both a borrower and a lender be. He or she will borrow at the beginning and save toward the end. They will gain from inflation (if any) when they are young and lose to inflation as they approach middle age. From their point of view, there is much to be said for this balance. From the point of view of the lending bank, inflation is not without its compensations. Inflation of real estate prices has the advantage of improving the quality of the bank's portfolio. Foreclosures will be fewer, and losses in each foreclosure will be lower. Taken by itself, inflation no more explains the S&L debacle than does the borrowing-short-and-lending-long story.

Now we reach the root of the matter: What devastated the S&Ls was a tremendous rise in the interest rate.

The first noticeable sign of things to come was a period of tight money in 1955–57, but no one expected the trouble we've seen. The federal funds rate in those years jumped from 1.78 percent to 3.11 percent, and continued to rise. By 1965 the average S&L was earning only 0.5 percent on its capital. Crises followed in 1966, 1969, 1974, and 1978. High T-bill rates and the new money-market mutual funds drained the S&Ls of deposits.

When on October 6, 1979, the new chairman of the Federal Reserve Board, Paul A. Volcker, announced that thereafter the Reserve would concentrate on the money supply and let the interest rate go as it pleased (it pleased to go up), the S&Ls' fate was sealed. In March 1980, the grandiloquently styled Depository Institutions Deregulatory and Money Control Act confirmed the seal. Practically unrestricted competition, coupled with $100,-000 deposit insurance, guaranteed that the savings and loans, trying to escape the consequences of high interest, would engage in a binge of blue-sky financing and outright thievery. The only surprise is that the binge lasted for a full decade before the general collapse.

But what could the Federal Reserve do? Doesn't inflation cause the interest rate to rise? When all is said and done, isn't the culprit the usual suspect—inflation? It's too bad—$500 billion too bad—that the S&Ls got caught in the crossfire of the Federal Reserve's war with inflation, but the war must go on, mustn't it?

Given the size of the S&L disaster, I suggest that the Reserve ought to have a pretty convincing explanation of the necessity for its actions. Chairman Volcker used to tell us that the interest rate was none of his doing but was the doing of the impersonal market. To the best of my knowledge, his successor, Alan Greenspan, has not said him nay. Well, if the Federal Reserve does not control the interest rate, I don't know what it does do — unless, as W. S. Gilbert sang of the House of Lords, it does nothing in particular and does it very well.

Of course, the Reserve claims to control the money supply. Its Federal Open Market Committee buys or sells government bonds (it could trade in other assets as well, but prefers not to). If it wants to contract the money supply, it sells government bonds until enough banks buy enough of them to reduce their cash reserves and hence their loan-issuing power. If it wants to expand the money supply (a stratagem that rarely crosses its mind) it buys government bonds and builds up the banks' reserves.

There's more to buying and selling than stamping your foot and saying that's what you want to do. Your price must be right. If you want to sell, your price must be enticingly low. A low price for a bond (or any asset) yields a high rate of return. Not only are banks eager to buy high-interest Treasury bonds, they are also quick to adjust upward the rates they charge their customers, whose credit, after all, is less solid than that of the U.S. government. In the same way, when the Open Market Committee buys bonds at a high price, it drives the interest rate down.

Because the money supply is not a precise figure (the Reserve publishes four different major and two minor ways of measuring it), the effects of this activity on the money supply are not precise. But the activity certainly does have determinate effects on the interest rate, and that certainly has definite effects on the cost of living.

All of which brings us back to 1951. In the preceding decade the Federal Reserve Board and the Treasury worked together to maintain the price of government bonds, and the prime rate for most of those years — despite their including World War II and the first year of the Korean War — remained steady (believe it or not) at 1.50 percent. In 1951 the Reserve, worried about inflation, managed to break free of the agreement with the Treasury and thereafter devoted itself to controlling inflation by managing the money supply.

As it happens, 1951 is the midpoint between the founding of the Reserve in 1913 and 1989, the most recent full year for the Consumer Price Index. Several fat volumes would be required for an exhaustive economic history of each period, and a thorough analysis of the impact of those histories on the CPI would be beyond reasonable achievement. Yet some events are clearly more significant than others. For obvious reasons, wars are held to be especially inflationary, while depressions are deflationary. World Wars I and II and the start of the Korean War occurred in the first period, while the Korean War truce talks and the Vietnam War occurred in the second period. The recession of 1920 and the Great Depression occurred in the first period, while there have been five (or six, if you count what's going on now) recessions in the second period. So we may say with some justice that the control of inflation should have been no harder in the more recent period—particularly since the Federal Reserve Board had now proclaimed this to be its primary objective—than in the earlier one.

How, then, do the two periods compare? From 1913 to 1951, the Consumer Price Index (1982–84 = 100) rose from 9.9 to 26, an increase of 163 percent. In the later period, from 1951 through 1989, the index rose from 26 to 124, an increase of 377 percent. In other words, during the thirty-eight years that the Federal Reserve Board has been deliberately and ostentatiously fighting inflation, the inflation rate has gone up more than twice as fast as it did in the previous thirty-eight years. On the record, the burden of proof is on the Federal Reserve Board to show that its policies, which have resulted in the destruction of the S&Ls, have been effective by any standard whatever.

As I have argued previously ("Bankers Have the Classic COLA"), a high interest rate causes rather than cures inflation. This will always be true because the outstanding nonfinancial debt in the nation is greater than the GNP. At the present time, the former stands at about $9.75 trillion, and the latter is about $5.4 trillion. Thus each percentage point in the interest rate is paid for by an increase of $97.5 billion in the general price level, while a 1-point increase in inflation costs only $54 billion. With interest rates currently running about 6 points above normal, this year's net cost of the Federal Reserve Board's inflationary policies will be $261 billion—or considerably more than the budget deficit everyone moans about.

In comparison, the cost of the S&L mess is small potatoes. Nevertheless, it must be added to the other costs the Federal Reserve Board is responsible for. Several presidents and Congresses have undoubtedly acted stupidly in regard to the S&Ls, but the S&Ls would still be operating and prospering to the benefit of us all if it were not for the stubbornly misguided behavior of the Federal Reserve Board.

[9/90]

What Happened to Jimmy Carter

James MacGregor Burns, Pulitzer Prize–winning biographer, historian, and political scientist, recently published *The Crosswinds of Freedom*, the third and final volume of his history of *The American Experiment*. The book confirms Burns's standing as one of the foremost observers of the modern American scene. It also carries forward the foreboding analysis he initiated in *The Deadlock of Democracy*: that American law, by creating a stalemate in politics, makes an almost impossible demand on—and for—leadership.

Jimmy Carter of course figures in *Crosswinds*, and reading about him makes you want to cry. He was (and is) a decent man who apparently thought decency was enough, who had a talent for offbeat public relations, and who also had a propensity for shooting himself in the foot. The prime example was the Iran hostage affair. As Burns points out, it was Carter who kept that in the news, and it helped defeat him. On the other hand, if not for Iran, Ted Kennedy might have been able to grab the Democratic nomination. The economic situation was probably enough to finish Carter, no matter what. In that connection I offer a footnote to Burns's magisterial book.

During the last two years of Carter's presidency we had double-digit jumps in the Consumer Price Index. It is not clear why this happened. The usual explanation blames OPEC. What is generally forgotten is that OPEC blamed the strong dollar for its price increases. For almost three decades—long before the advent of Paul Volcker—the Federal Reserve Board and other First World central banks had been steadily pushing interest rates higher, thus overhauling their currencies and raising the cost of the goods the OPEC members (which generally had few resources aside from their oil) bought from us. Before raising their prices, OPEC tried for several years to persuade us to change our policies; but the Reserve plowed ahead, increasing the federal-funds rate from 4.69 percent in March 1977 to 6.79 percent in March 1978 and to 10.09 percent in March 1979.

Finally, on March 27, 1979, OPEC oil went up 9 percent, to $14.54 a barrel, and three months later there was another jump of 24 percent. In December OPEC was unable to agree on a uniform price, but individual hikes were made across the board. By July 1, 1980, the barrel price ranged from $26.00 in Venezuela to $34.72 in Libya. Thus, in a little over a year, the cost of oil had more than doubled.

Yet petroleum accounted for less than 3 percentage points of the inflation. Moreover, in every OPEC year (and, indeed, in every year on record), the nation's interest bill has been substantially greater than the national oil bill (including domestic oil and North Seas oil as well as OPEC oil). If OPEC is to blame for the inflation of 1979–81, the Federal Reserve Board is even more to blame.

A major cause of the rest of it was hoarding, which resembles speculation yet differs from it in that real things are involved. During this period the stock market was quiescent: The price/earnings ratio was lower than it had been at any time since 1950, and less than half what it would be in 1987, or is today. But hoarding, probably prompted by memories of the gas lines following the 1974 OPEC embargo, was heavy.

And not merely in petroleum; it extended to all sorts of commodities. Manufacturers, wholesalers, retailers, and private citizens tried frenziedly to protect themselves against expected shortages. As often happens in such situations, the expectations were immediately self-fulfilled. Confident that shortages would allow them to raise prices, manufacturers eagerly offered high prices themselves for raw materials they needed. Maintenance of market share became an almost obsessive objective of business management.

In the book business, for example, "defensive buying" became common. Bookstores and book wholesalers increased their prepublication orders for promising titles so that they would have stock if a runaway best-seller developed. Publishers consequently increased their print orders to cover the burgeoning advance sales. It soon became difficult to get press time in printing plants, and publishers increased press runs for this reason, too. Naturally, everyone also stockpiled paper, overwhelming the capacity of the mills. For all I know, the demand for pulpwood boosted prices of chain saws and of the Band-Aids needed by inexperienced sawyers.

Unlike speculation, hoarding has physical limits. After a while, there's no place to put the stuff. And after a while, the realization dawns that a possible shortage of oil and gasoline doesn't necessarily translate into an actual shortage of historical romances. Moreover, the shortage of oil and gasoline, once the tanks were topped off, disappeared. There was plenty of oil and gasoline; you just needed more money to buy it. Hoarding—or most of it—slowed down and stopped. Business inventories declined $8.3 billion in 1980. But prices didn't come down.

All this time Jimmy Carter was not idle, for he prided himself on being what we've come to call a hands-on manager. As early as July 17, 1979, he got resignations from his Cabinet members and accepted several, including that of Treasury Secretary W. Michael Blumenthal. To fill the Treasury slot, he chose G. William Miller, chairman of the Federal Reserve, and that opened the spot for Paul A. Volcker, who was nominated on the 25th amid cheers on Wall Street. At his confirmation hearings on September 7, Volcker revealed the conventional wisdom to the

House Budget Committee. "The Federal Reserve," he testified, "intends to continue its efforts to restrain the growth of money and credit, growth that in recent months has been excessive."

True to Volcker's promise, on September 18 the Reserve raised the discount rate from 10.5 to 11 percent; and then, less than three weeks later, from 11 to 12 percent. An additional reserve requirement of 8 percent was imposed on the banks. More important, a fateful shift to monetarism was announced. The Reserve, Volcker said, would be "placing greater emphasis on day-to-day operations of the supply of bank reserves, and less emphasis on confining short-term fluctuations in the Federal funds rate." On February 15, 1980, the discount rate was set at 13 percent.

Despite this conventionally approved strategy, prices kept going up. In January and February, the inflation rate was 1.4 percent a month, or about 17 percent a year.

Again President Carter took action. On March 14, 1980, using his authority under the Credit Control Act of 1969, he empowered the Federal Reserve Board to impose restraints on consumer credit. It immediately ordered lenders to hold their total credits to the amount outstanding on that day. If they exceeded that amount, 15 percent of the increase would have to be deposited in a non–interest-bearing account in a Federal Reserve Bank. The banks and credit-card companies, adopting various procedures, hastened to comply.

All that was good standard economics. If inflation is caused by too much money, the obvious cure is to reduce the amount of money. President Carter and Chairman Volcker were in complete agreement.

The new policy had an immediate effect that, surprisingly, surprised the president and the chairman. Not only did sales slow down, as expected, but profits did, too—as should have been expected. The automotive industry cried hurt almost at once. General Motors reported an 87 percent drop in profits, and Ford and Chrysler reported losses. The housing industry saw trouble coming as well. It even appeared that consumers were taking seriously their leaders' pleas to cut down consumption: Some credit-card companies found their cardholders responding to restrictions by borrowing less than now permitted.

Alarmed by these and other complaints, the Reserve relaxed the new regulations after two and a half weeks, cut the reserve requirements on May 22, lowered the discount rate on May 28, and abolished the credit controls on July 3, whereupon the president rescinded the Board's authority to act. It was all over in three and a half months, in plenty of time for the nominating conventions. Everyone pretended to be pleased with the result, and in fact the inflation rate did fall, but not below the double-digit range. Still, Carter had shown that he could "kick ass" (his phrase), so he won renomination. His hope of reelection, though, was dashed.

As Jimmy Carter moved back to Plains, Georgia, he must have wondered why inflation remained high. The OPEC turbulence had subsided. Hoarding had largely stopped. Cutting consumer purchasing power had brought on instant recession.

Conventional theory has taught us to look at the money supply, or the budget deficit, or the trade deficit in seeking an explanation for inflation, since it is supposed to follow when these are high and going up. Well, M1, the measure of the money supply the Federal Reserve claimed to control, went from 16.8 percent of GNP at the start of Carter's term down to 15.3 percent at the end. Carter's reputation as a spendthrift notwithstanding, the budget deficit, again as a percentage of GNP, was lower in every one of his years than in any one of Ronald Reagan's. As for international trade, the deficit on current account was four and a half times greater in Reagan's first term than it was under Carter, and of course in the second term it pierced the stratosphere—where on a clear day it can still be seen.

Carter's mistake—and the mistake of the American people—was the common one of simply accepting what someone says he or she is doing. Everybody, including the Federal Reserve Board itself, believed its contention that it was fighting inflation by encouraging the interest rate to soar. Meanwhile, in the last two years of Carter's term the nation's interest bill went up 51 percent, although the outstanding indebtedness increased only 23 percent. In addition to the fall in M1 that we've noted, the Board increased the federal-funds rate 68 percent and the New York discount rate 59 percent. In 1951 (when the Reserve started its well-publicized wrestle with inflation) it took only 4.59 percent of GNP to pay all domestic nonfinancial interest charges. The Reserve pushed the rate up, in good years and bad, until it stood at 15.04 percent at the end of Carter's term. (It's much higher now.)

It is generally recognized that Volcker slowed inflation (he obviously didn't stop it) by inducing a serious recession, (if not depression) in 1981–83. Putting aside the question of whether causing so much grief was a noble idea, we may ask how pushing the interest rate up caused the recession. The answer, of course, is that it made goods too expensive for most consumers. Standard economics, though it pretends the consumer is supreme in the marketplace, perversely believes that consumption is a bad thing.

Goods became unaffordable for two reasons. On the supply side, interest is a cost of doing business; so the prices businesses charged had to cover all the usual costs, plus the cost of usurious interest. On the demand side, interest is a cost of living; so the prices consumers could afford were reduced by the interest they had to pay. Usurious interest pushes prices up and the ability to pay down.

Had the interest rate not risen, wages would probably have risen. Unemployment would certainly have fallen. More people could have bought more things. More producers could have sold more things. Prices might have gone up until people could no longer afford to buy; but if so, that stage would not have been reached so quickly or so inexorably as with usurious interest. And those who had money to lend would have been worse off, unless they were wise enough to invest their money in productive enterprise or spend it on consumption.

Would instant Utopia have been achieved? Of course not. The point is that the conventional policies of Jimmy Carter and Paul Volcker were good for lenders but bad for everyone else.

The tests of a "sound" economy that people still chatter about—a stable money supply, a balanced budget, and a favorable trade balance—all were worse under Reagan than under Carter. Inflation was worse under Carter—and defeated him—because the interest rate was higher. Professor Burns rightly fears that we will not find leaders able to organize power to handle the usual social and international problems. I fear that we are even less likely to find leaders capable of understanding and leading us out of the slough of conventional economics.

[11/89]

In for a Penny, In for a Pound

In October 1987, just before the stock market crash, one Peter G. Peterson had an article in the *Atlantic* that caused a lot of talk on commuter trains. Peterson was President Nixon's secretary of commerce in 1972. He astutely left the Cabinet the following year, and has since been an investment banker as well as a tireless agitator in the press and on TV. He was as responsible as anyone for the 1983 boost in Social Security taxes and the partial tax on Social Security benefits. He continues to talk darkly about "entitlements," to warn that universal medical care will be the death of us, and to plead for a tax on consumption.

After reading Peterson's article, I started to do a column on what's wrong with it, but it would have taken a year's worth of this space. One sentence has nevertheless kept nagging at me. I quote: "We now know, for instance, that a maximum tax of 50 per cent actually generates more revenue from the wealthy than a maximum rate of 70 per cent, and provides real incentives for budding entrepreneurs." This claim was in furtherance of the claim that it would be a mistake to ask the wealthy to pay for their share of the deficit. It calls to mind an Artemus Ward saying I treasure: "It ain't so much the things we don't know that get us in trouble. It's the things we know that ain't so."

By an aberration of my W. C. Fields–like filing system, I can lay my hands on one, but only one, set of old tax instructions. We can make do, however; it's the top bracket Peterson is talking about, so we'll talk about that too. When we mention the incomes of the wealthy, we'll mean just the part of their incomes that is taxed at the top rate — 70 percent or 50 percent, as the case may be.

It will be convenient to have a minimum high income. Peterson doesn't give one, but let's guess that to count as wealthy in his book, one has to have $200,000 in the top bracket.

We also need some ground rules. I'll name two: (1) The differences we're going to consider will not have anything to do with tax shelters, because Peterson speaks only about the tax rate, and anyhow shelters are greatly restricted by the 1986 law; and (2) inflation won't have anything to do with our calculations either. We want a level playing field, as the *Wall Street Journal* would say.

Now, as I read Peterson, he seems to be saying that if you take all the $200,000-and-up incomes as above defined, add them together, and tax them at 50 percent, you will collect more taxes than you would if you taxed them at 70 percent. That's too preposterous for anyone to believe; surely Peterson must have meant something else. Let's explore the possibilities, for he seems to think he's hit upon a great social truth.

We'll start with a little algebra. We will call x the amount taxed at 70 percent, and y the amount taxed at 50 percent. Then if taxes paid in the two years are equal, our equation would be $0.70x = 0.50y$. Solving the equation for y, we have $y = 0.70x/0.50$, or $1.4x$. In other words, the amount taxed at 50 percent would have to be at least two-fifths greater than the amount taxed at 70 percent.

The mathematics is unimpeachable, but perhaps Peterson is focusing on something different. Low rates are often said to take the incentive out of cheating on taxes. I'm no economic determinist, so I don't hold with that. Indeed, in spite of recent studies funded by the IRS, I'll stand right up and say that half of the wealthy taxpayers are honest. And why not? As the chorus sings in *Iolanthe*, "Hearts just as pure and fair/May beat in Belgrave Square/As in the lowly air/Of Seven Dials." Then for every honest wealthy taxpayer who reported an income of $200,000 in both years, there would have to have been a wealthy cheat whose income was really $360,000, who didn't report $160,000 of it when the rate was 70 percent, but who cheerfully reported it all when the rate fell. In that way, the wealthy as a class would report 1.4 times as much at the lower rate as at the higher, and the total taxes paid by them would remain the same.

Is Mr. Peterson telling us that that many of the wealthy are dishonest? And if he believes that, does he believe the cheaters would suddenly become honest once the marginal rate dropped? Having spent even a year in Nixon's Cabinet, he can't believe that. To quote *Iolanthe* again: "In for a penny, in for a pound."

Let's try another approach. It has been said at least since the New Deal days that high taxes sap the incentive of producers to produce. After a certain point, they are supposed to get tired of working for Uncle Sam; so they quit working, or maybe take longer lunch hours. This is thought to be bad for everyone because these people are, by definition anyway, the most productive among us. We should try to get them working again by allowing them to hold on to more of what they get their hands on.

Ronald Reagan used to tell, with feeling, how high income taxes in his movie-star days made it not worth his while to make all the flicks he could have. One of the roles he turned down was the one Humphrey Bogart played in *Casablanca*. Who says high taxes are all bad?

To keep a level playing field, we'll consider only what is called earned income, for increased interest or dividends or rents would go also to remittance men, who know nothing of incentives since they do nothing anyhow. To be sure, our big-time producers are used to getting much of their income from stock options and such, but the 1986 law, by taxing capital gains as ordinary income, has largely eliminated that particular incentive.

Although the morals are slightly different, the mathematics of the incentive argument is the same as the mathematics of the cheating argument. So I ask: Does Peterson mean that our can-do people will increase their doings by 40 percent just because the tax rate has been cut? Does he want us to believe that they're doing whatever it is they do without half trying? Does he think it honorable of them to have done this (quoting *Iolanthe* yet again) "By taking a fee with a grin on [their] face/When [they] haven't been there to attend to the case"? Or put it this way: If they lack incentive to do what they're supposed to, why don't they get out of the way and let someone else do it?

Well, I'll make another guess at what Mr. Peterson meant. Maybe he's saying the incentive of a lowered tax rate will boost thousands of people from the $150,000 class to the $200,000 class, which would now have more members and consequently a higher total income.

This explanation is more plausible than the others, and there actually was a highly unrepresentative sample of its possible effect in the sports pages of the *New York Times* the other day. In 1985, when the tax on the wealthy was, well, too complicated for me to explain, there were five ballplayers with annual wages in excess of $2 million. In 1986, when the rate is somehow lower, there are ten in the golden circle. With twice as many making $2 million, their rate could fall in half, and the total taxes paid by those poor chaps would remain about the same. Is this what Mr. Peterson meant?

If so, he didn't mean much. The five new boys were all making well over a million last year; so it took only raises of a few hundred thousand to double the number of players in the $2-million bracket and thus double the taxes paid by the superstars. This is what is known, among less exalted players, as bracket creep and is mostly due to inflation, which we agreed to rake out of our playing field.

It doesn't really make any difference what reason Peterson gives for the behavior of the wealthy. The fact remains that if they paid more taxes after a 50 percent rate than they did after a 70 percent rate, their marginal-rate income had somehow to go up at least 40 percent. A $200,000 income taxed at 70 percent had to become at least $280,000 taxed at 50 percent. And that's not all. Their pre-tax income went up at least 40 percent. But their after-tax income jumped 233 percent, from $60,000 to $140,000 (and under the new tax law will jump again — to $190,-000 or more).

Peterson is a great sleight-of-hand artist. He wants us to keep our eyes on the taxes paid, and not notice the jump in disposable income. This is the way multimillionaires are made. As the tax rate was cut, there came a great leap forward of executive salaries and perks, of lawyers' fees and doctors' fees, of tax shelters and arbitrage deals, of interest rates and capital gains. These leaps account for the tax collections Peterson celebrates. There weren't any million-dollar-a-year ballplayers before the cut, and few others with that kind of income. By 1985 (the latest figures in *Statistical Abstract of the United States*), there were some 17,000 Americans in that fast-growing class. As Phil Rizzuto would say, that's not too shabby.

On another level, it's very shabby indeed. For if Peterson is right in his figures even though vague in his reasons, the maxi tax cuts gave enormous gifts to the wealthy and nibbled away at the incomes of everyone else. Now, I'm going to throw a lot of figures at you to show you what's happened in the ten years and I beg you to be careful how you use them. They come from *Economic Report of the President, 1988.* Some are in 1986 dollars, some in 1977 dollars, and some in current dollars, but within each category the figures are comparable.

First, remember the poor. In 1977 there were 5.3 million families, or 31.7 million people, living in poverty. By 1986, the numbers had risen to 7 million and 34.6 million, respectively.

Next look at average weekly nonagricultural, nonsupervisory earnings (1977 dollars). In 1977 they were $189.00 and had fallen to $169.28 by 1987. The average annual earnings of the lucky ones who worked a 52-week year were $9,828 and $8,802, respectively. The 1977 figure was slightly above the poverty level, the 1987 figure considerably below it. Of course, those who didn't work full time didn't do so well.

Then consider the median family income (1988 dollars). This was marginally up, from $31,252 in 1977 to $31,796 in 1986. Note that a two-earner family, working full time, wouldn't come close.

Finally, consider the after-tax income of the median families (this is where the wealthy shone like burnished gold). In 1986 dollars it fell, from $25,443 in 1977 to $24,095 in 1986. When you include the increase in Social Security taxes (largely engineered, as aforesaid, by Peterson), the fall was much greater.

In short, from 1977 to 1986, poverty was up a third; weekly earnings were down 10.4 percent; the median income was up 1.7 percent; but the after-tax income of the median family was down 5.3 percent. And the after-tax incomes of the wealthy more than doubled. This is what Peterson and his ilk are fighting for. They profess to be very worried about the deficit and are ready even to admit that it grew because of the tax cuts. But they don't propose to give up those cuts. No, they want us to put all that behind us. They want us to look ahead to a sales tax (which they call a consumption tax), because such a tax falls very little on them but very much on the middle class, especially the lower middle class, and on the poor.

I think these people know very well what they do.

[6/88]

New Ways to Get Rich

During the last few years a new fungus has swollen in the dark of
the financial moon. This is the securities futures market, or markets, the most prominent of which trades guesses about the future of the Dow-Jones Index. This trading is said to be similar to
that on the commodities exchanges, where you can bet on the
future price of sugar or platinum or orange juice; but the
similarity is superficial.

If I were crazy enough or shrewd enough to play the commodities markets, I'd go in for pork bellies, because this solemn
game appeals to my sense of the ridiculous. The unit of trading
is a contract to buy (or sell) 40,000 pounds of the stuff (which I
suppose is a carload—a carload of book paper is 40,000 pounds)
at a specified price at some future date. That's a giggling amount
of bacon to bring home.

As I write this, the price for next March is 63.40 cents a pound.
Suppose you buy a contract to buy and, come March, the price
is 73.40 cents a pound: You sell your contract at that price and
pocket the difference, or $4,000, less a trifling brokerage charge
and taxes. You don't have to feed the pigs; you don't smell them
or hear them squeal; you never even put up any real money; and
you can sell any time you think the price is right. You just pick

up a piece of change for guessing right. Of course, if you guess wrong, you take a bath in the trough.

The commodities markets are gambling dens for millionaires. Conscience-stricken brokers (there are some such) claim that the trading stabilizes prices and so helps farmers plan. We don't have to take that claim seriously to see that, in the end, someone winds up with some actual bacon to sell to someone else who has not been persuaded by Jane Brody to give up ingesting animal fats.

The stock market futures are something else. What is traded there is the right to buy a bundle of stocks, which are already a couple of markets away from something you can get your teeth into. After all, the stock market itself is claimed to stabilize the cost of capital and so help General Motors to plan production. Again, this is a claim we don't have to take seriously. But when we read in the business press the claim that the futures market stabilizes the stock market, which stabilizes the cost of capital, we know we are in the land of make-believe. Why not a market in options to buy futures, thus stabilizing the futures market?

Now, it is true that stock market futures have some slight appeal to people engaged in productive enterprise. Enterprises deal with the future all the time anyhow. The local bookstore orders its Christmas stock in July; the publisher sent the manuscript to press in January; the printer and paper manufacturer have to order their machines years ahead.

It takes time to do business, and during that time the prices of things change unpredictably. If you contract today for a $10-million warehouse to be ready a year from now, you worry that by that future date the real estate market may have tumbled so that your competitor can buy one standing empty for $8 million and thus be in a position to underprice you. You may worry so much that you decide to hedge your bet, which you can do by selling stocks short. Then if prices fall, the money you gain by selling short will offset the value lost on the warehouse. And if prices rise, the increased value of the warehouse will offset the money lost on the stocks. Obviously, when you hedge a bet, you narrow your possible gains as well as your possible losses; and you may be ready to do this because you want the warehouse to do business in, not to speculate with.

The stock futures market is an organized way of selling short and so is convenient for businessmen with heavy commitments they'd like to hedge. Once the market is in operation, it offers a field day for big-time gambling on a sure thing. For various reasons, a gap will open from time to time between the futures market and the prices of the underlying stocks. When the gap is big enough (maybe only a point or two), arbitrageurs will buy in the cheaper market and sell in the dearer. It's a riskless gamble, but you have to act fast, and you have to have access to an enormous amount of money to make the game worth the trouble and expense.

The gaps that open between the markets are not exactly the doings of the famous invisible hand. Those who run futures markets pride themselves on developing what they call "products" that will appeal to traders. (It would be hard to imagine anything less like a tangible product or more airy-fairy than the chits that are traded.) A successful "product" — one that has, as they say, a great deal of sizzle — is one that is extra volatile. The more volatile the markets, the bigger the possible gaps. The bigger the gaps, the more trading. The more trading, the more volatility.

The other day a vice-president of the New York Stock Exchange, which usually pictures itself as sedate and conservative, gave a TV interview in which he talked pretty smugly of a new "product" the exchange is pushing. This is the Beta Index. Stocks that are highly volatile are said to have a high Beta characteristic, and the Beta Index is a weighted average of the 100 most volatile stocks on the exchange. Beta Index futures, it is hoped, will be not only volatile but sizzling. There'll be big gaps for sparks to jump.

Trading to take advantage of gaps is an old way of making money. It has a better claim than Marx's elaborate analysis to be the method of primitive accumulation that made capitalism possible. In *The Wheels of Commerce,* the second volume of his trilogy *Civilization and Capitalism, 15th–18th Century,* Fernand Braudel makes much of the fact that the first large Renaissance fortunes were made in long-distance trade. The money wasn't made in haulage; the function of distance was to open gaps in information and consequently in prices that enabled experienced and well-informed traders to buy cheap and sell dear. Like the arbitrageurs of today, they used other people's money: partnership funds, bank deposits, and ultimately credit, some of it not unlike junk bonds. Fortunes accumulated very fast.

What fascinates people about stock index futures is that the big trades are dictated by computers, which still, when they aren't "down," have an aura of magic. It's all done in seconds, as compared with months or even years a half millennium ago. On a recent day, some 40 million shares were traded in the last few seconds before the market closed. Only eight or ten years ago, 40 million shares made a big day on Wall Street; and on Black Tuesday in 1929 only 16,410,000 shares were traded. Today's buy and sell orders are programmed, which seems different from human agency (though programmers are presumably human). But the principle is the same. Also the same is the uneasiness aroused in the breasts of ordinary citizens by the extraordinary winnings of the traders.

The uneasiness is certainly justified. The old curse (variously said to be Chinese, Jewish, or Hungarian) can be paraphrased to read, "May you live in volatile times." Yet the stock exchange itself could scarcely exist if it were not inherently volatile. It is disingenuous or ignorant to claim, as many do, that the market is an efficient way of valuing the nation's industries. There is much fluttering in economic dovecotes if the GNP varies in a year as much as 2 percent from its secular trend line; but the stock market can rise or fall that much in a single day.

In a rational world, the value of a nation's industries would be a function of what they produce. In the world of Wall Street, the nation's industries are merely an occasion or an excuse for buying and selling pieces of paper. What is being valued is not the corporations that issued the paper but the traders' guesses about what the Federal Reserve Board will do next. An offhand remark by the chairman will trigger a bigger rise or fall in the market than any conceivable news about actual production. Indeed, favorable news of production is likely to cause the market to fall, because it is thought likely to frighten the Board into raising the interest rate in order to try to exorcise the inflation banshee. Commentators will intone a few traditional homilies about the effects of high interest rates on industry, but what really matters is that a rise in the interest rate reduces the capitalized value of every income-earning asset.

The business press is fond of pointing out that everyone who guesses the Board is in a good mood is matched by someone who guesses it's in a foul mood. Otherwise there wouldn't be any trading. The implication is that the shaking and baking all evens out and doesn't matter.

Unfortunately, it does matter. Several trillion dollars are now committed to stock futures and other "derivatives." These trillions are invested in "products" that neither are products nor produce products; they are denied to productive industry or to government investment in schools, colleges, medical care, and the infrastructure of the economy.

Not so long ago, college endowment funds, pension funds, and the like were invested almost exclusively in high-grade bonds. Bit by bit they all have been seduced into playing the market, where they are managed by "experts" with an eye to churning the accounts and so picking up a fraction of a point here or there, day after day. It can all add up, just as a vegetable market makes a tiny profit on sales but a tidy profit on investment by turning its inventory almost daily. Given the record, it will not be surprising if the managers of these funds are tempted by the stock futures markets, where the winnings can be two or three times those of the stocks themselves.

As this comes to pass, more and more of our money will be frozen in nonproductive speculation. The resulting Ice Age will leave our industries, of which we were once justifiably proud, high and dry.

[9/86]

Go and Catch a Falling Dollar

Aside from false pride, why do we worry when the dollar falls a bit? Two answers are given: (1) We don't want to scare foreign investors into pulling their marks and yen out of our economy, and/or (2) we don't want to do anything to start inflation again. Quick rejoinders are: (1) There are dollars but no marks and yen in our economy, and (2) no one who has had occasion to buy anything thinks inflation has ever stopped. Let's take a look at the problem in a little more detail.

Those foreign investors were a big concern of former Federal Reserve Board chairman Paul A. Volcker. The story was that we needed them to finance the budget deficit because, as pundits keep telling us, we don't save enough to finance it ourselves. And the foreigners, being strangers in a strange land, had to be offered bait in the form of high interest rates. It is possible to argue that our maneuver was self-defeating, since the annual interest on the federal debt is now close to double the annual deficit. Yet mistake or not, the bonds have been sold, some with coupons as high as 15.75 percent, and there is nothing that can be done about it; so we should (as politicians plaintively plead about a great many things) put it behind us.

At this point we are supposed to worry that foreigners will pull

out if the dollar falls much lower, and it is certainly understand-
able that the Great Crash of 1987 may have made them skittish.
Getting their money out could, however, be a bit more complicated than it appears.

Say Mr. Togo has some of those nice 15.75 percent twenty-
year bonds (payable November 15, 2001) and so does Ms. Falck,
and they want to sell them. No problem. The quote this morning is 153 bid, 153⁶⁄₃₂ asked. Although the price may shift a bit one
way or the other by the time our foreign friends reach a bank or a
broker, they can be confident of selling the bonds at 153, give or
take a few cents. Cents? Well, yes, and naturally the 153 is dollars. They'll get $15,300 for each $10,000 bond they own—a nice
capital gain on top of the 15.75 percent interest they've been re-
ceiving since purchasing the bonds in 1981.

But Mr. Togo and Ms. Falck don't want dollars and cents.
The whole idea is to pull their money out of the United States,
because the financial tipsters they read tell them Washington
isn't going to put its house in order (whatever that means). They
want good old yen and marks, respectively. Again, no problem.
This morning the yen is quoted at 127.90 to the dollar, and the
West German mark at 1.6805 to the dollar. There may be a slight
fluctuation before the exchange is made; still, Mr. Togo and Ms.
Falck will have their familiar currency back.

Now, when Mr. Togo and Ms. Falck are given yen and marks
for their dollars, it is because someone buys their dollars for yen
and marks. Obviously. But look you: The numbers of dollars,
yen, and marks remain the same (this is one place where money
has a quantity). Mr. Togo and Ms. Falck can get their money out
only if some other foreigners put theirs in.

Should all foreigners try to get their money out simultaneously, the exchange rate of the dollar would surely fall, and
fall very fast (this is the one place where the law of supply and
demand works). It wouldn't be a free-fall. At some stage Mr.
Togo's compatriots would get so few yen for their dollars that,
say, $40 million wouldn't be worth much to them, and they
might just as well use it to buy a painting of flowers that van

Gogh never got around to finishing. Or Ms. Falck's compatriots might think it smart to buy an American publishing house or two with their cheap dollars.

In the end, the only way all foreigners can get their money out of the States is by buying something we have to sell. Of course, this is how they got the dollars in the first place: We bought some of what they had to sell. It is also well to remember that, budget deficit and all, ours is a pretty stable society and therefore not altogether a bad place to keep your money. Moreover, our debts are denominated in dollars (except for some worrisome ventures of our biggest borrowers), which distinguishes us from Third World debtors.

The pressure is not all one-sided. We're eager to buy Hondas and BMWs, and they're eager to buy American securities, both public and private. They may not be so eager to buy more securities if the Federal Reserve lets the dollar continue to fall, but they'll have to buy something we have to sell—unless they intend to give us Hondas and BMWs for free.

They may buy goods we produce, and that will certainly be fine with us. On the other hand, they may buy or build factories to make a Stateside version of the Honda. Or they may put their excess dollars into real estate. Large chunks of our major cities are already Japanese owned, just as large chunks of London are Arab owned (and substantial pieces of Manhattan are British and Canadian owned). Patriotic sentiment aside, should we be upset by foreign investment in American industry and real estate?

From the standpoint of American working men and women, it makes no difference who their employers are (unless they're self-employed) so long as the employers are fair and decent. From the standpoint of American consumers, it makes no difference who produces the merchandise they buy so long as the quality is good and the price is fair. From the standpoint of American investors—well, they've shown themselves more interested in speculating on the stock market, anyhow. From the standpoint of the American government, taxes on foreign-owned income could be as good as taxes on domestic-owned income (I say "could be" because the Bush administration wimpishly restored breaks for foreigners that we've canceled for ourselves).

There remains the problem of the profits earned by these foreign-owned factories and buildings. Our payments to foreigners are already in the tens of billions of dollars annually. If they go even higher, won't they drain the lifeblood out of the economy? Hardly. These profits are in dollars and thus only exacerbate the foreigners' difficulty in converting dollars to yen or marks or whatever. The profits will have to be spent on American goods or invested in American industries or exchanged for yen or marks at increasingly unattractive rates.

Mr. Togo's and Ms. Falck's last option is worth a moment's notice. It is their ultimate option; and if the dollar continues to fall, it won't be worth much. In an unexpected way it will fulfill Keynes' prophecy of the "euthanasia of the functionless investor." As Keynes explained in the closing chapter of *The General Theory:* "Interest today rewards no genuine sacrifice, any more than does the rent of land. The owner of capital can obtain interest because capital is scarce, just as the owner of land can obtain rent because land is scarce. But whilst there may be intrinsic reasons for the scarcity of land, there are no intrinsic reasons for the scarcity of capital."

Unfortunately for Mr. Togo and Ms. Falck, capital denominated in dollars is overabundant and will accordingly be ill paid. (It happens to be overabundant in their homelands, too, but that's not our worry.) Of course, Mr. Togo and Ms. Falck still have the penultimate option of leaving their money where it is, in which case there is no need for the Federal Reserve Board to "defend the dollar."

Because dollars will mean so little to them, our Japanese and German friends will be increasingly able to outbid us for paintings and publishing houses and such that come on the market. That will be a blessing for those of us who have things for sale, but it brings us to the second problem of the falling dollar — inflation.

Conventionally, inflation is seen to result from the rising dollar cost of imports. The effects are both direct and indirect. Directly, to the extent that the price of a Mercedes is a factor in the Consumer Price Index, an increase in the number of dollars it takes to buy a Mercedes tends to increase the CPI. Indirectly, if it becomes necessary to put up $85,000 worth of marks to import a Mercedes, General Motors might feel safe in bumping the price of a Seville. There is little in the history of General Motors to suggest a reluctance to do the bumping, nor can I think of any likely reason for them to hang back.

Potentially more serious are increases in the costs of raw materials, principally oil. The effect here is somewhat mitigated by the fact that OPEC quotes its prices in dollars. It is also mitigated by the fact that sluggish economies around the world have made oil a glut on the market. It could be further mitigated, if not eliminated, by the pursuit of rational conservation policies — but that's probably too much to expect us to undertake.

The inflationary effect I call your attention to is the bidding up of the prices of American industries. That happens when companies are bought outright and also when shares are bought on the exchanges. The Great Crash of 1987 is one sort of consequence. A much more dangerous consequence is the compulsive reaction of American managements to increased valuation of their companies. They feel obligated — and indeed are obligated by their investment bankers — to try to raise profits to match the increased valuations. They can do this in two ways, neither of them desirable — by raising prices, which is inflationary, and by holding down wages, which is stagnatory.

In the space remaining I can only suggest that the conventional solution of protecting the dollar by raising interest rates is precisely wrong-headed: It is merely another prescription for stagflation. The hopeful solution would combine a monetary policy of low interest rates (which would tend to encourage industry) with a fiscal policy of steeply progressive taxation (which would tend to discourage speculation by foreigners as well as by Americans).

If such a solution incidentally soaked the rich, it's about time, for it must be acknowledged that they have not performed faithfully as stewards of the inordinate share of the common wealth they have engrossed over the past fifteen years, and especially over the past seven. Their wanton misuse of their increased riches mainly to create a bull market and a crash was, and is, a passionless prodigality.

[2/88]

Junk Bonds and Watered Stock

In the 1920s, bond salesmen were admired and envied. Later, when Wall Street laid its egg, they became butts of bitter jests ("Where are the customers' yachts?" asked a book by Fred Schwed, Jr.). In the end, they were objects of opprobrium and scorn. Today's bond salesmen seem to be following in their grandfathers' footsteps.

Today's salesmanship is marvelously subtle, combining an ancient rhetorical device with an even more ancient childhood game. Long before Aristotle wrote his *Rhetoric*, Greek sophists found that an appearance of frankness could help them win a bad case, and that they could get good marks for sincerity by openly admitting a superficial weakness or two. And since long before the sophists, children have known how to tempt their peers with the challenge "I dare you."

The device and the game are combined in the term "junk bonds." The immediate connotation is of shoddy goods or a tangle of broken and rusty machinery, old plumbing fixtures, and wrecked automobiles, an unsightly mess, partly hidden by a tumbled-down board fence as unsightly as what it pretends to hide. A secondary connotation is of junk mail, which almost everyone hates. Take a vacation, and on your return you will fill garbage cans with the stuff. If you're on one mailing list, you're on them all.

The junk-bonds metaphor boldly accepts these connotations and so disarms criticism. No one, it winks, is trying to fool anyone.

At the same time, these bad connotations are modified by some that are at least ambiguous. Those who send out junk mail presumably think well of it. Paraphrasing Abraham Lincoln, one might conclude that God must love churches and charities that raise money by mail, since He made so many of them. For another example, junk food is eaten by an awful lot of people, who apparently have tolerance, if not taste, for it; and purveyors of junk food make an awful lot of money, which is something the purveyors and buyers of junk bonds hope to do, too.

Besides all this, the term admits risk and so suggests sport. I dare you to run the risks that may lead to a big killing. Are you big enough to afford such risks? You say that the capitalist system depends on risk taking: Do you dare put your money where your mouth is? In the great game of life, where's your sporting blood?

But just as a paranoiac may have real enemies, junk bonds may be really bad. They may not necessarily be bad for the new owners of the corporations that issue them or for the purchasers or for the underwriters, but they are almost invariably bad for the corporations themselves, and they are undeniably bad for the morale of our society and bad for the tax collections that support our society.

In spite of all the talk, junk bonds are not new. Practically all railroads issued bonds at usurious rates—and ultimately paid the penalty. Nor are junk bonds the first securities of "less than investment grade" to be widely marketed in the United States. Most of our giant corporations—including many of those now being raided—were originally papered together with such securities. The chosen instrument was different, and the metaphor was different, but the results were similar. Stock was issued instead of bonds, and the stock was said to be watered—like cheap whisky.

In *Other People's Money*, Louis D. Brandeis, later Supreme
Court justice, told how the United States Steel Corporation was
formed in 1901: "The steel trust combined in one huge holding
company the trusts previously formed in the different branches
of the steel business. Thus the tube trust combined 17 tube mills,
located in 16 different cities, scattered over 5 states, and owned
by 13 different companies. The wire trust combined 19 mills; the
sheet steel trust 26; the bridge and structural trust 27; and the
plate trust 36. . . . Finally, these and other companies were
formed into the United States Steel Corporation, combining 228
companies in all. . . ."

The tube trust, when it was put together a few years earlier,
had been capitalized at $80,000,000, half of which was common
stock, and half of which common "was taken by J. P. Morgan &
Co. and their associates for promotion services; and the $20,-
000,000 stock so taken later became exchangeable for $25,000,-
000 of Steel Common." The tubes plainly held a lot of water,
and so did all the other trusts that went into United States Steel.
Nor was this all. The rest of Steel Common was watered in its
turn, and nearly one-seventh was issued directly or indirectly to
the promoters.

Brandeis doesn't give all the gory details, and I don't have a
research assistant to work them up, but I suggest to you that at
least half of the original 228 companies were enticed to sell out at
greatly inflated (or pumped up) prices. Some of the others may
have been squeezed a bit, but the total paid for the 228 was almost certainly far greater than their total net worth. When you
add it all together, you have the United States Steel Corporation,
the first corporation capitalized at a billion dollars, and pretty
close to half of it was water.

In Morgan's time, high-flying corporations were overcapital-
ized. Today they are undercapitalized, a.k.a. leveraged. The differences are not differences of style, reflecting the personal idi-
osyncrasies of T. Boone Pickens, who seems not to mind being
called a shark, in contrast with those of J. P. Morgan, who bra-
zenly painted his yacht black and named it *Corsair*. The differ-

ences, instead, are a function of the tax laws.

When U.S. Steel was floated, there was no corporation tax. Since earnings were not taxed, interest paid on bonds was obviously not deductible. Interest was a fixed expense. Dividends, on the other hand, were not fixed (except for some on preferred stock). You paid dividends when you were flush; otherwise not. Therefore a prudent company got its money from stock, not from bonds. Today, with the corporation tax at 46 percent (assuming a corporation pays any taxes at all), and with interest payments deductible, a clever company will issue bonds instead of stock, and a clever raider will happily issue junk bonds paying 14 or 15 percent in order to buy up stock earning 5 or 6 percent. After the deduction, the new load on the company is only 6 or 8 percent, and before it becomes oppressive, the raiders will be long gone.

That the debt will eventually become oppressive, there is usually little doubt. The flow of interest payments will have to continue in bad times as well as in good. If profits fall or disappear, so will the benefit from deductibility. The corporation's cash flow will be soaked up by the high interest payments. Even a sluggish cash flow can quickly lead to bankruptcy. Of course, bankruptcy may now be sought in order to break a labor contract, whereupon the company may become solvent again. Guess who's left with the short end of the stick?

This result of undercapitalization is, you may be astonished to learn, not substantially different from the result of overcapitalization. How was the water in Big Steel paid for? As the man might say, there's no such thing as a free drink. If the capitalization was half water, Steel's earnings on its real assets would have had to be twice "normal." Without that research assistant, I can only suggest the outline: First, the owners of the original 228 companies were well paid. Second, J. P. Morgan and his fellow underwriters were *very* well paid. Third, those who bought the watered stock got "normal" dividends. Fourth, the price of steel was not grossly exploitative (steel rails stayed at $28 per long ton for more than ten years).

At this point, someone is sure to claim that U.S. Steel was more efficient than its 228 components had been. Evidence for this is the fact that most of the 228 were shut down, and that those remaining were expanded. But a question nags at me: If those shut down were inefficient, why were they bought in the first place? Isn't the competitive system supposed to let inefficient companies die?

The case for technological efficiency is, if anything, worse. In 1911, ten years after the flotation of U.S. Steel, *Engineering News* reported: "We are today something like five years behind Germany in iron and steel metallurgy, and such innovations as are being introduced by our iron and steel manufacturers are most of them following the lead set by foreigners years ago." (This might have been written yesterday.)

The question remains: Who paid for the water? Those of you who didn't immediately answer "Labor!" will stay after class and be given a quick review of the effects of mass immigration, Taylor-system management, and courts that issued injunctions against labor unions as conspiracies in restraint of trade.

Since the Civil War days of "Betcha Million" Gates and Jay Gould, speculation has resulted in American enterprises' paying too much for capital. Andrew Carnegie, who had some hands-on experience with such matters, observed in *The Empire of Business* (1902), "The efforts of railway managers to-day are . . . directed to obtain a return on more capital than would be required to duplicate their respective properties." It matters little whether the capital is paid for with dividends on watered stock or with interest on junk bonds. Either way, it is the working men and women—the people who put that capital to work—who do the ultimate paying.

[3/86]

Why Not Meet the Payroll?

A recent editorial in the *New York Times* opened with these words: "Michael Milken is a convicted felon. But he is also a financial genius who transformed high-risk bonds—junk bonds—into a lifeline of credit for hundreds of emerging companies. Snubbed by the banks, these businesses would otherwise have shriveled. . . . There is no condoning Mr. Milken's criminality. But if overzealous government regulators overreact by dismantling his junk-bond legacy, they will wind up crushing the most dynamic parts of the economy."

This reminded me of a story about Henry J. Raymond, the *Times'* founding editor and a member of Congress. One day he was prowling the House floor, trying to arrange a pair on an important upcoming vote, so he could return to New York on business. Old Thad Stevens (one of my heroes) asked, "Why doesn't the gentleman pair with himself? He's been on both sides of the question already." Raymond's successors seem to be straining to be on both sides of the junk-bond question.

For my part, I'm ready to grant that Milken is (or was) a crackerjack salesman and a mighty cute operator. But a financial genius he was not. Certainly he was not the first investment banker (what an impressive-sounding job description!) to sell carloads of not-of-investment-grade securities (see "Junk Bonds and Watered Stock"). Nor is the *New York Times* the first journal to discover virtue in such supersalesmanship. Nor, I daresay, is this the first time the *Times* itself has made such a discovery. Junk bonds are a slight variation on a very old theme, played at least as early as the Mississippi Bubble and the South Sea Bubble, both of which burst in 1720.

I'm also ready to grant that a lot of emerging companies have been snubbed by banks, yet I rather wonder why. Having paid casual attention to some banks' advertising campaigns, I was under the impression that nothing was more likely to make a banker's day than an opportunity to lend a helping hand to a bright but inexperienced young woman with a new idea for a flower shop, or to a similarly energetic young man eager to play a part in the great drama of American business. If the banks weren't seizing these opportunities, what were they doing with the money they persuaded us to deposit with them?

Well, one thing they did was make Milken's junk-bond business possible. They were no big buyers of junk bonds themselves (although the savings and loans snapped up about a tenth of those issued). Instead, they supplied bridge loans. When Robert Campeau made his deals to buy the Allied and Federated department store chains, he did not put up much cash. He counted on selling junk bonds, and he knew that would take a little while, especially since it was important to wait for the moment when the market was right. The banks loaned him the money to bridge that gap. After the bonds were sold, the banks would be paid off, handsomely.

The trouble was, it turned out that the junk couldn't be sold, at least not at the necessary price; so the banks involved couldn't be paid off. They were stuck with nonperforming loans, and Campeau's stores took refuge in bankruptcy. One of the banks went bankrupt, too. Junk bonds aren't doing a job the banks are falling down on; the banks are in fact doing the job indirectly by making all those bridge loans. The banks are essential players in the junk-bond game.

Not surprisingly, the Federal Reserve Board (which is responsible for the availability of credit) doesn't see a problem here, anyhow. The Board has just reported: "There is little evidence that a 'credit crunch' is developing; the majority of businesses say they have not seen any change in credit terms and have had no trouble getting credit. Where credit tightening by banks and thrift institutions has been noted, however, it has mainly affected newer small businesses and the real estate industry." A medical researcher would scorn that diagnosis as anecdotal. It doesn't mean much to say a "majority" of businesses have no trouble with credit; 49 percent could be having a lot of trouble.

Whatever the situation, we can be sure that the "newer small businesses" turned away by the commercial banks are also unable to find an investment banker ready to float junk bonds for them. The junk-bond market being thin and precarious, a $3-million issue is about the smallest anyone will undertake. This assumes a company with upwards of $15 million or $20 million in annual sales. It is not the sort of stuff that made Milken notorious, but it is considerably more than can be expected from most newer small businesses.

A new small business has always had a tough time and always will, for the reason suggested by John Maynard Keynes. "If human nature felt no temptation to take a chance," he wrote, "no satisfaction (profit apart) in constructing a railway, a mine, or a farm, there might not be much investment merely as a result of cold calculation." Every new enterprise faces a high probability of failure.

Real estate, though, is a key industry. New Building Permits Issued is one of the "leading indicators" of the economy. No prosperity lasts long if real estate does not prosper. Moreover, we have great need of it. Not only do we have uncounted millions of homeless and ill housed; we are unable, in this supposedly family-oriented society, to provide enough affordable housing for young couples, employed and upwardly mobile though both partners may be.

Still, as everyone knows, real estate loans are prominent

among the troubles of savings and loans and of commercial banks like the one pushed past the brink by the Campeau fiasco. Why do the loans go bad? Not because the housing is not wanted or not needed, and only partly because prices are too high. It is the high carrying charges that are to blame. Real estate loans go bad for the same reason junk bonds go bad. The interest rates are usurious. The usury affects real estate developers (another impressive job description) and contractors as well as potential buyers, and commercial construction as well as residential. High interest rates are a main factor of high real estate prices—and of high furniture and food and clothing prices, too.

Interest charges paid by the nonfinancial sectors of the economy are now in excess of 20 percent annually. They were only 4.9 percent of the GNP in 1950, rising to 7.2 percent in 1960, to 10.1 percent in 1970, and to 15.0 percent in 1980. These great leaps forward, culminating in today's 20 percent, didn't just happen. They were carefully fine-tuned by the Federal Reserve Board.

Why did the Board members do it? They have certainly told us enough times. They've been fighting inflation. Unfortunately, the fight has not been remarkably successful. You can see that from the fact that the Consumer Price Index, which stood at 24.1 in 1950, reached 126.1 forty years later—an increase of 523 percent. (As I've remarked before, this figure seems to me too low; the food, clothing, shelter, transportation, education, medicine, and entertainment I buy have all increased much more than that. But let that pass.)

High interest becomes a self-fulfilling prophecy. What is prophesied is the probable failure of the borrowers. The probability is a risk the lenders must protect themselves from. They protect themselves by charging even higher interest. That, naturally, increases the risk of failure.

Abstractly there is no end to the escalation of interest rates, for there is no end to the escalation of risk. Indeed, in a sort of Malthusian progression, risk increases geometrically while rates increase arithmetically. Actually, of course, the escalation does have an end, because potential borrowers are driven off. That may be prudence, but foreclosing production (or consumption) does not make for prosperity.

It all comes back to the nation's monetary policy—its rates and rules and regulations. Deregulation, combined with tightened credit, results in escalation of rates. Escalation of rates discourages production and encourages speculation. Junk bonds are just one of the forms speculation takes. Junk bonds are the creation of the nation and of the Federal Reserve Board (which is, absurdly, an independent power), not of the genius of a super-salesperson.

There is another issue here. The *Times* thinks that junk bonds are good because they force companies to become more efficient (and hence more "competitive") in order to pay off the high interest charges. If this tale isn't false, I wish somebody would cite a few shining examples.

There are certainly examples on the other side, Allied and Federated department stores being first among them. Both chains were long established. I know, because in the days of my youth I spent many goldbricking hours waiting in their sample rooms to see buyers. They were also successful. They're not successful now.

Furthermore, the usual test of efficiency is a fat bottom line, and the quickest way to fatten the bottom line is to fire some people and put a leash on the rest. But as John Kenneth Galbraith argued years ago in *The Affluent Society*, an economy that makes life unpleasant for people is something we don't need. If the virtue of junk bonds is that they are a sort of handicap inspiring efficiency, why not try a different handicap by giving all the working stiffs a raise? It used to be said that management's first test was meeting the payroll. Why wouldn't meeting a bigger payroll be a better test than paying higher interest?

[4/90]

Economists Can Be Bad for Your Health

We are told the real trouble with our health-care system is that it doesn't conform to economic principles. Our objective, economists say, should be to make it subject to market discipline. The dense complexity of the Clinton plan, particularly all the stuff about managed competition, was intended to achieve this end.

I'm not sure that analysis of the problem makes much sense. For one thing, the principles economists talk about with such a lofty air don't have a lot to do with our sublunary world. For another, market discipline is precisely what the medical profession, together with its ancillary services, is subject to right now.

We Americans are a judgmental people; so let's talk about discipline first. Market discipline is a childishly simple idea. If it means anything at all, it means that if you won't buy what I have to sell, I can't sell it to you. To this there is a corollary: If I won't sell what you want, you can't buy it from me. Price obviously is a factor in both the proposition and the corollary. The local jeweler has many diamond necklaces, and I have many daughters and daughters-in-law, and Christmas is coming; but we can't get together on a price. Well, everyone understands that.

It is, however, argued that health care is different from diamond necklaces, that one is a life-or-death necessity, while the other is, as the doctors say, elective. This is true, up to a point. Putting aside the fact that, if Perry Mason is to be believed, more than one murder has been committed for a diamond necklace, we know that food, clothing, and shelter also are certainly life-or-death necessities. Indeed, one of the shames we all bear is that many of our fellow citizens forgo medicines doctors have prescribed for them because they need their pittance for food. That's market discipline. Have you noticed that the pharmaceutical houses learn the lesson and lower their prices? And the food companies? The poor, some thirty-six million of us, have already learned that (as a Depression-era love song had it) to be broke, kid, is not a joke, kid, it's a curse.

In short, "market discipline" is just a couple of words put together to make readers of the *Wall Street Journal* feel toughminded and virtuous. The doctors can't sell more heart surgery because they're already overworked, and besides, their prices are too high for the market, but they're making out all right. The drug companies have not been altogether spared the disciplinary rod, but it's been wielded by politicians, not by the market.

Many people fuss that doctors have an "uneconomic" advantage because they can increase their profits by ordering more and fancier tests and requiring their patients to stay longer in the hospital (presumably to test whether they're too far gone to complain about the food). I fuss about all that, too; but I also fuss that I can't buy an automobile without a radio, and that motel restaurants insist upon serving (and silently charging for) fried potatoes or grits, *garni de persil*, with my breakfast egg. This is what used to be called block booking in the movie theater business. Actually, though, it's all simply good old-fashioned American market discipline, otherwise known as doing as much as you can get away with.

In the news lately there has been a beautifully apposite example of market discipline enforced by the most sacred of economic laws, the law of supply and demand. A pharmaceutical company makes a drug that is used for deworming sheep. Since the company has been making the item for nigh onto thirty years, it's got the manufacturing down pat and is able to earn a profit charging the shepherds six cents a dose, which is evidently all that market will bear. A doctor at the Mayo Clinic had an idea that the drug might be useful in controlling colon cancer in humans. The clinic conducted tests, at its own expense, then the Food and Drug Administration reviewed the findings and approved the drug for human use. The manufacturer turns out roughly the same supply as before, but the demand is now enormous; so what is the price for colon-cancer sufferers? Only six dollars a dose.

That's market discipline for you again. What would you expect? The supply is unchanged but the demand is way up; so "naturally" the price goes way up, too. In fact, the price naturally goes up faster (and further) than the demand, because the demanders are not all of the same intensity. Some are more eager than others, and a few may be desperate.

It used to be said that you could get a parrot through the orals for a Ph.D. in economics by teaching it to repeat "supply and demand" (a less pregnant rejoinder than "Nevermore"). In our time there has been, as Nobelist Gerard Debreu says, "a change from the calculus to convexity and topological properties." This change has probably held down the supply of economists (no parrots need apply), and possibly increased their price, but it has not modified the vacuity of the law of supply and demand.

There are two essential points to understand about the alleged law. The first is that the economy doesn't work the way economists imagine it does, and never has. The market, howsoever you want to define it, doesn't set prices. How could it? It's not alive. It can't say even as much as a parrot. No trade occurs until a price is set by a human being or by a corporation of human beings and is accepted by another human being or corporation. The buyer may set the price (as in an auction) and the seller may accept it, or (as usually happens in ordinary business) the seller may set the price and the buyer may take it or leave it. Either way, both buyer and seller are free and responsible. Both are making a statement: "We are the sort of people who act like this."

That statement, I would suggest, is comparable to the statement made by a high-school sophomore wearing a baseball cap backward in a lunchroom. I am not trying to make fun of anyone. The statements of buyer and seller and cap-wearer may not be clear and unequivocal, but they are perfectly serious. More than that, they are necessary and unavoidable. We are what we do. We understand ourselves only by what we do and by others' responses to our doings. We cannot escape history, and we cannot escape making statements.

Which leads us to the second essential point about economic laws: Economics is a branch of ethics, not of natural science. If economics were a science, there would be no responsible way to point a finger at a six-dollar price for six cents' worth of deworming medicine. As a matter of fact, scientific economists from Karl Marx to Milton Friedman would agree that whoever set that price had no choice. He or she was only responding to market discipline, to the law of supply and demand. Being merely a response to a stimulus, the price was neither right nor wrong. It might have been set in the same way that a dog salivates at the sound of a bell.

But it wasn't a dog salivating. The person who set that price was making a statement. It might have been something like "I'm getting mine while the getting's good." Or "This is a crummy thing to do, but I don't dare get the stockholders mad at me." Or "A windfall profit here will enable us to underwrite that desperately problematical investigation we discussed this morning." Or the statement might have been something quite different. I don't know enough about the case even to make a guess. But I can tell you this: The person making the statement was either enlarged or diminished thereby, and the law of supply and demand had nothing to do with it.

I don't understand why we are so anxious to set up a health-care system too complicated for anyone to explain in order to impose an illusory "market discipline" on the medical profession by getting a handful of giant insurance companies in competition with each other. We already know how that sort of competition works in the pharmaceutical industry. In health insurance it's no different.

From the point of view of the consumer, insurance companies can be judged by their "loss ratio"—the total of claims paid divided by premiums charged. A high loss ratio is favorable to the consumer; a low loss ratio means that policyholders pay in much more than they get out. Among the companies that hard-sell their medigap policies on television, the loss ratio is usually a little below or a little above 50 percent. The loss ratio of the policies Prudential writes for the American Association of Retired Persons is 78 percent; group policies written by the other big companies are in the 70s, but not quite so favorable to the consumer as AARP's.

And what about Medicare, that obviously bureaucratic do-gooding government agency? Conventional wisdom insists that private enterprise can always run rings around the government. But Medicare's loss ratio is in the 90s. In other words, the market discipline imposed by competition among giant insurance companies costs the consumer at least 20 percent more than a government-run single-payer system.

The reasons for the relative efficiency of Medicare are plain enough: (1) It has no marketing expense, while the private insurance companies spend billions on salespeople and on advertising to back them up. The competing entities of Clinton's scheme will have similar selling expenses, for competing requires selling. (2) Private companies have to maintain reserves against unexpected surges of claims, and so will the Clintonian entities. Medicare, relying on the full faith and credit of the federal government, has no such need. (3) Lean and mean though the private companies may be, their scores of assistant vice-presidents would turn up their noses at the pay and perks of the *head* of Medicare.

The final irony is that true-blue conservatives attack President Clinton's plan as the proposal of a true-blue liberal. Actually, it is the middle-of-the-road proposal of a middle-of-the-roader. The president's program is certainly better than what the conservatives have proposed, but my mother always warned me that it wouldn't greatly improve my health to play in the middle of the road.

[12/93]

In Pursuit of a Fiscal Fantasy

President Clinton's $31-billion "stimulus package" was defeated by a filibuster that was organized not on the reasonable ground that the package was woefully inadequate, but on the fanciful ground that by increasing the deficit it would hurt the recovery now supposed to be under way.

Suppose we had an adequate stimulus—something on the order of $200 billion, rather than the proposed $31 billion. That kind of money could knock 5 points off the official unemployment figure, bringing it down to an arguably tolerable level of 2 percent, and could start to do a job as well on those who are working part time or are too discouraged to look for work.

But could we afford it? Of course we could. The late Arthur Okun, a universally respected economist and the chairman of the President's Council of Economic Advisers under LBJ, maintained that a 1 percent rise in unemployment causes a 3 percent fall in real national product. If Okun's law works backward and becomes a multiplier (not guaranteed), the 5 percent fall in unemployment we're after should result in a 15 percent rise in output. That would be about $850 billion and should, in turn, yield about $210 billion in taxes at present rates—not to mention the gains for state and local governments, or the savings in reduced welfare outlays. So our massive stimulus could produce a modest reduction in the deficit. As Mr. Micawber would say, result happiness.

The result would still be far from misery even if Okun's law didn't quite work backward, and even if the government proved incompetent in all the ways the naysayers say it is. If we had to borrow the entire $200 billion, the deficit would be increased by the interest, or by $13 billion—and if the Federal Reserve Board should miraculously decide to play on the same side as the rest of us, the interest could be as low as $4 billion.

Are you worried silly about the $16,750 that rabble-rousers say is your share of the national debt? Grow up. I have a $75,000 mortgage that I'll not pay off if I live till I'm 105. The bank isn't worried. My estate will pay it off, of course, and whoever buys the house will mortgage it again and will no doubt later refinance the mortgage to pay for some improvements or repairs. And so on. It's a well-built house and should last (and be mortgageable) for another hundred years or more. All that's necessary is for the successive owners to be able to pay the interest. The same is true of the United States of America and its national debt.

What is the alternative? It is proposed that we get government out of the way or off business's back or whatever metaphor appeals to you, and let the present "recovery" rip. The good old free enterprise system, we are told, the very system our economists are teaching with such smashing success to Russia and Eastern Europe, would soon show that a man knows what to do with his money a lot better than some bureaucrat in Washington. You bet.

The big trouble with this prescription for prosperity, worked out years ago by the classical economists, is that it is based on unrealizable assumptions. One assumption is full employment. A second is that a level playing field, of the kind the *Wall Street Journal* pines for, isn't enough. The players must have at least fairly equivalent equipment. Adam Smith put it this way: "The whole of the advantages and disadvantages of the different employments of labor and stock must, in the same neighborhood, be either perfectly equal or continually tending toward equality."

In addition, there's an assumption that economists pretend doesn't matter. All the buyers and all the sellers are assumed to know all about all the products available and the demand for them. Whoever believes this assumption should have followed me around last week as I shopped for a new automobile. I don't even know how to kick the tires. A contemporary school of economists gets rid of this assumption with another, namely, that everyone acts rationally and rationally expects everyone else to act rationally, too.

If you accept each of the assumptions, you probably can see some sense in the notion that an invisible hand will guide us to the recovery of our dreams. Don't be too sure. If I really knew what I was doing when I shopped for a car, I'd make the best buy possible—and so would you and everyone else. One dealer would start to get all the business. Then the competitors would lower their prices, and pretty quickly there would be one big price war.

Short of collapse, there could be no end to such wars. All competitors can lower their prices by cutting their costs. Their costs are someone else's prices, which likewise can be lowered by cutting costs. And so on ad infinitum. David Ricardo and his followers argued that this regress would be stopped by the costs of food and other basic things (called "wage goods") that workers need to survive.

But the costs of wage goods are not immune to cutting, so the regress would continue. Very likely some people would lose their jobs as prices tumbled, although the classical theory merely calls for wages to fall. Either way, if the free market were left to its own devices, the price-cutting, cost-cutting, payroll-cutting, demand-cutting sequence would continue unabated until prices, payrolls, production, and profits all approached zero. The free market could not stop the process—nor, if they played the game by the rules, could any of the participants. The invisible hand pushes everyone and everything inexorably down.

The drama has a different ending in the scenario of Léon Walras, the patron theorist of free market analysis. He wrote that "production in free competition, after being engaged in a great number of small enterprises, tends to distribute itself among a number less great of medium enterprises, to end finally, first in a *monopoly at cost price*, then in a *monopoly at the price of maximum gain.*"

So take your pick. The Walrasian theory has free competition ending in monopoly. The more conventional theory, though it says nothing about an end, offers no reason why general disaster should not result.

There is, of course, a third outcome—what actually happens. For we take steps to prevent disaster, either by accident or by design, and those steps reveal that we are, by turns, do-gooders, pragmatists, and sponsors of crime.

In our role as do-gooders we enact child labor laws, minimum-wage laws, worker-safety laws, social welfare laws, and many other laws to mitigate the horrors of free competition. It is not bad to do good—except in the eyes of conventional economics. In his speech launching the idea of a natural rate of unemployment, Milton Friedman condemned all altruistic measures. They would, he said, increase the natural rate of unemployment. Pre-depression America, which knew very little of such things, is touted as a time of low unemployment. It was also a time of child labor, the twelve-hour workday, labor injunctions, and similar amenities.

It must be confessed that we are more comfortable thinking of ourselves as pragmatists than as altruists. In any event, whereas businesspeople applaud the pronouncements of conventional economics, very few act in accordance with them. They may compete vigorously, but very few compete primarily on price, having learned (as a book of business advice once had it), "Don't sell the steak. Sell the sizzle." With less pressure on prices, there is less pressure on costs.

Finally, we are sponsors of the crimes we deplore. A character in the funnies used to say, "Crime don't pay well." For most practitioners that may be true, but it pays enough above the bottom of the current legitimate pay scale to entice hundreds of thousands into making a career of it. If these people were to renounce housebreaking and carjacking and mugging, and were to look for decent work, their competition for jobs would push the legitimate pay scale even lower.

And that's not all. As John E. Schwarz and Thomas J. Volgy show in grim detail in *The Forgotten Americans*, there are thirty million working poor in America—people who are desperately trying to live the work ethic yet still cannot afford the basic necessities at the lowest realistic cost. Heartbreaking thousands of these people take a flier at drug running or prostitution just to survive.

We are, as I say, sponsors of all this crime and squalor. It serves to retard the free-fall of the economy, and with our altruistic and pragmatic practices it will eventually help us to settle at a stopping point somewhere between here and the pits. Economics, however, takes time, and it will be years before we reach that point. When we do reach it, we will find ourselves in what economists call an equilibrium, with upwards of a quarter of our productive capacity unused, with twenty million of our people unemployed or underemployed, and with probably fifty million men, women, and children living lives that are far from solitary but are nevertheless (in the rest of Hobbes's phrase) poor, nasty, brutish, and short.

I don't suppose that, aside from a few fanatics for the apocalypse, there is anyone who is eager for such an equilibrium. But there are many millions who are capable of denying its possibility, and (as with other diseases) the denial makes its actuality the more deadly—especially since conventional economics can think of no way to upset the equilibrium, except by doing more of the same.

In the past, similar equilibria have been upset by wars. The Civil War made us a nation; World War I industrialized us;

World War II got us out of the Great Depression. Professor Joseph A. Schumpeter celebrated the creative destructiveness of great new industries, like the railroads, which rendered canals obsolete, and the automobile, which doomed the horse-and-wagon. (Some expect the computer to play a similar role, but the information revolution is responsible for much of the payroll cutting currently in progress, including its own.)

The thing about these equilibrium upsetters—these wars and these creative destroyers—is that they've all required ever bigger expenditures by ever bigger government. The expenditures for war are obvious; but often forgotten are the grants of public land to build the railroads, together with the postal contracts to keep them running, and the paving of streets and building of highways for the automobile. Is it conceivable that we can summon the wit and the will to make the expenditures that need to be made today?

I cannot conceive it. What is all too probable is that the welfare of the nation and of increasing millions of our fellow citizens will continue to be sacrificed to an accounting fantasy called a balanced budget.

[6/93]

Starving All the Way from the Bank

To write this I had to turn off a television show featuring a rock star, eyes closed in rapture or agony (it was not clear which), moaning an expression of his solidarity with the people starving to death in Africa. I should—and shall—leave the task of commenting on TV performances to Marvin Kitman. I will even resist the temptation of recalling the Stan Freberg skit of a few years ago in which he asks everyone to stop at a certain hour of a certain day and tap-dance for peace.

There is no question that our fellow citizens' capacity for pity and terror has been stirred by the pictures they have seen of the starvation in sub-Saharan Africa. There is no question that they want to help in some way. It would be pretty to think of them beginning by wondering how the tragedy came about. For anyone ready to take that necessary initial step there is a book available called *Debt Trap: Rethinking the Logic of Development*. Yes, I am afraid that to understand starvation in Africa you must start with money and banking, because they are the roots of the problem.

The author of *Debt Trap* is Richard Lombardi, a former vice-president of the First National Bank of Chicago. His office was in Paris, a nice place to have an office, but he was in charge of lending in both French-speaking and English-speaking Africa, and he traveled widely and steadily in those countries. What he saw troubled him deeply, for he is an intelligent and compassionate man. To think about the situation in greater depth he took a leave of absence and became a research associate and Thursday Fellow in Georgetown University's School of Foreign Service. The result is his important and enlightening work.

Lombardi lays out the connection of starvation with banking roughly as follows: People starve because they cannot get food. They cannot get food because they either do not grow it or have no means of securing it from those who do grow it. In Africa they do not grow so much food as they used to, since many farmers have moved to the city and many more have switched to crops for export, like sugar and coffee and cola nuts. Their governments have induced them to switch to export crops to earn foreign exchange. The governments need foreign exchange to try (unsuccessfully) to meet the interest payments on their foreign loans.

Why do they have foreign loans? It comes down to Gertrude Stein's answer when she was asked why she had written *Tender Buttons:* "Why not?" As Lombardi tells it, the world's big bankers bought the oil sheiks' OPEC winnings on the Eurodollar market and then jet-setted around the Third World peddling the money. The bankers called this recycling; actually, it was salesmanship.

The bankers happened to launch their maneuver at about the time that the Third World nations, almost without exception, were in trouble with the World Bank and the International Monetary Fund. The bankers could offer assistance because they had money and also because they had a new vision—not of banking, but of what they came to describe as "world financial enterprise." Lombardi credits (if that is the right word) this vision to Walter Wriston, who transmogrified the First National City Bank of New York into Citicorp in 1967. At any rate, the "Citicorp Concept" was reverently discussed in the business press and widely emulated by David Rockefeller's Chase Manhattan and the rest. The hairy details I'll leave you to read in Lombardi's book, only noting Wriston's fatuous dictum, "But a country does not go bankrupt."

The stage was now set. The Third World needed (or wanted) money; the bankers had it (or knew where they could get it). And the bankers had convinced themselves that all Third World loans were risk free. What happened? In 1960, Lombardi tells us, Third World debt totaled $7.6 billion. A quarter of a century later, it was nearly $1,000 billion—that is, $1 trillion, or an increase of roughly 12,000 percent. The sum was not owed to the banks alone. U.N. agencies are heavily committed, as are our Export-Import Bank and its counterparts in other First World nations.

All of this occurred because those who count in both the First World and the Third World have been acting out what Lombardi (using an unlovely but fashionable word) terms a "paradigm." Two components of the paradigm are Ricardo's Law of Comparative Advantage and the notion that a growing GNP cures all ills. A third principal component, perhaps not now so prominent as the others, is the theory of Walt Rostow (Lombardi erroneously calls him Walter) that developing societies invariably pass through five stages: "the traditional society, the preconditions for takeoff, the takeoff, the drive to maturity, and the age of high mass consumption."

In the grip of this paradigm, everyone began pushing the Third World to modernize and industrialize. Our Export-Import Bank and its ilk underwrote sales of steel mills and sugar refineries and atomic energy plants. The national airlines of countries of fewer than a half million souls, most of them tribesmen with neither the need nor the possibility of flying anywhere, bought fleets of Boeing 747 jumbo jets. The World Bank lent money at low rates for roads and airports and dams and other infrastructure. The U.N. "Development Decades" favored an urban focus, precipitating a population shift from farm to city. The demand for agricultural exports accelerated the shift, because export crops tend to be more efficiently handled by agribusiness than by customary methods.

Under such prodding the Third World's GNP rose even faster than the Development Decades had hoped. But Third World debt rose faster yet. This outcome, which should be a puzzle to true believers in the GNP, threatened to swamp the U.N. agencies. The IMF (then as now) counseled austerity, meaning cut imports (or, more frankly, reduce your standard of living) and expand exports (done by lowering wages and, again, your standard of living).

At that point in time (as Watergate taught us to say) the Citicorp Concept flashed across the horizon. Gone was the old-fashioned bankerly attempt to evaluate the business prospects of each enterprise applying for a loan. In its place was the actuarial notion that lots of risks are safer than a few. Risk itself disappeared because countries did not go bankrupt. Recycling could go on merrily as long as Third World countries could be induced to borrow money at a point or two over what the bankers had to pay for it on the Eurodollar market.

It turned out not to be difficult to induce Third World countries to borrow, what with everyone advising them to do so and especially with fewer and fewer questions asked. Lombardi has some horror stories to relate. A billion-dollar steel mill in Nigeria is too sophisticated to use the low-grade ore it was originally intended for. Zaire has the longest transmission line in the world, and no particular need for it at either end. A loan to Costa Rica was underwritten by a banking syndicate on the basis of a one-paragraph news article in *Time*.

At least some of the borrowers were foolish like fox terriers. They didn't bother to buy so much as a new presidential palace with the money, instead sending it straight to numbered bank accounts in friendly Switzerland. Periodically, statesmen who had that kind of foresight were overthrown, and their successors opened up their own numbered accounts. No one knows how many billions thus disappeared. The critical fact, however, is that the bankers lending the money didn't care; they lent the money to countries, not to individuals, and countries don't go bankrupt, even when they are stolen blind.

Of course, countries whose debts have increased 12,000 percent in twenty-five years do usually have trouble meeting even the interest payments. So the IMF urges austerity; food is in short supply; starvation looms—chronic starvation, not the sort that results from a natural disaster.

Lombardi paints the unhappy picture with great fervor. He emphasizes that the Third World's troubles are not merely those of an exploding population. The population problem certainly plays a role, but in the improbable event of zero population growth troubles would remain. The key is breaking the paradigm.

Lombardi suggests ways this can be done. He also shows the trouble the paradigm has caused and will cause in the First World—that is, to you and me. For when bankers lend money to Brazil to buy a steel mill or to Tunisia to manufacture blue jeans or to Singapore to keypunch data into American computers via satellite, Americans lose their jobs.

The apostles of the Law of Comparative Advantage (a.k.a. "free trade") counter that building the Brazilian steel mill and the Tunisian garment factory and the Singapore data-processing equipment makes jobs for Americans, and to a degree they are right. An hour or two at, say, John F. Kennedy Airport in New York will convince you that Boeing has sold (with Export-Import Bank help) an awful lot of 747s to foreign airlines you never dreamed existed. Still, unless we are prepared to give our airplanes and steel mills and wheat and corn away, someone has to pay for them—that is, the loans the bankers have made for us have to be paid off. If they can't be paid off, our friendly bankers will surely find ways to transfer the bad debts to us taxpayers. And if they are paid off, Third World austerity programs will throw Americans out of work. "When bank credit to Mexico stopped in 1982," Lombardi observes tellingly, "more jobs were lost in the following six months in the United States than in the three previous years of a depressed U.S. auto industry."

Banking, in short, is not an innocent enterprise. It can cause starvation in the Sudan and unemployment in Cincinnati. Faulty practice flows from faulty theory. Faulty banking theory flows from faulty reading of history.

[5/85]

Playing the China Card

Well, we decided to play the China card again. A more limp, greasy, shapeless piece of cardboard could scarcely be imagined. We have been waving it around for the past two hundred years, so it is no wonder that it has become too tattered for anyone to be sure what (if anything) it actually is.

From the beginning, we have had three ideas about China: It is "very large," as Noel Coward put it; there must be a lot of souls there for missionaries to save; there must be a lot of people there who want what we have to sell, whether their souls are saved or not. We have been right on number one.

The first American traders landed at Canton in 1785, three years before the ratification of the Constitution. The first American tariff act, passed on July 4, 1789, gave goods imported from China and India substantial preferences, provided they were shipped in American bottoms. During the ascendance of the China clippers (1833–69) and for the rest of the century, American trade with China was second only to that of the British, but was still very small. As a result of the British-instigated Opium War (1839–42), the Chinese opened several additional treaty ports, not only to the British but also to all other traders, thus themselves laying the basis for what would become Secretary of

State John Hay's Open Door policy. In 1867 the first American ambassador to China resigned in order to represent China, and shortly negotiated a treaty with Secretary of State William Henry Seward giving Chinese most-favored rights to visit, travel, and reside in the United States.

Amid this and much other similar activity, U.S. traders and missionaries grew increasingly conscious of their great distance from home and from American bases. Consequently, when the Spanish-American War suddenly put the Philippines in our hands there was a rudimentary China lobby ready to support the imperialists led by Theodore Roosevelt and Henry Cabot Lodge, who pushed for annexation.

President William McKinley was puzzled about what to do. "I went down on my knees," he explained subsequently, "and prayed to Almighty God for guidance more than one night. And one night late it came to me . . . that we could not turn the [Philippines] over to our commercial rivals in the Orient—that would be bad business and discreditable. . . . There was nothing left for us to do but to take them all, and to educate the Filipinos, and uplift and civilize and Christianize them, and by God's grace do the very best we could by them, as our fellowmen for whom Christ also died."

And so we got bases from which we could try to protect our trade with China, immediately fought a shameful two-year war with Emilio Aguinaldo to hold on to them, and simultaneously became embroiled in the Boxer Rebellion in China. At that time our trade with China represented 0.10 percent of our GNP. The corresponding figure today, after three major wars (plus two decades of expensive, futile, and domestically divisive support of Chiang Kai-shek), is 0.12 percent.

That 12 hundredths of 1 percent, President Bill Clinton assures us, means 150,000 jobs, and he may be right, although he also boasts of adding 250,000 jobs each month, and that's enough to scare the Federal Reserve Board silly. On the other hand, our imports from China, now four times our exports, must mean 600,000 jobs lost. No doubt we had already shipped most of them to Pakistan, Hong Kong, or Singapore. As a jolly Wall Street textile analyst told the *New York Times*, "If American retailers did not get cheap dresses from China, they would get them from Mexico, or, hey, Vietnam."

John Stuart Mill spoke of the value "of placing human beings in contact with persons dissimilar to themselves, and with modes of thought and action unlike those with which they are familiar." There is, accordingly, talk of how our traders will educate the Chinese in the ways of market capitalism. Recent events in Russia and Eastern Europe have muted that talk somewhat. Recent events in the United States should shut it off entirely, for it's hard to equate lean and mean downsizing and part-timing, the most prominent feature of contemporary American business, with human rights. And, indeed, businesspeople are nearly unanimous in rejecting even voluntary human rights guidelines for trade with China.

The China card of course has a purely political side. The game President Clinton has been playing set seven conditions for renewal of China's most-favored-nation status, with two declared mandatory. The first mandatory condition was that China must abide by its 1992 agreement not to export prison-made products to the United States. It's not clear that the Chinese have done much abiding, but the president has done a small part of it for them by excluding Chinese guns and ammunition from the most-favored-nation privilege.

I'm not sure whether we are going to bar Chinese guns and ammunition altogether or whether we are going to charge high tariffs; but no matter, it looks like another slap in the face of the poor old National Rifle Association. Yet I can't help wondering whether it may not be a briar patch the NRA wants to be thrown in, because the big supporters of and contributors to the NRA are American gun and ammunition manufacturers; in comparison, the good ol' boys are (so to say) spear carriers. It's heartwarming to see these defenders of the Constitution willing to protect their employees from having to compete with Chinese political prisoners, even though it means that the good ol' boys who are their customers will have to pay more because Wal-Mart will be able to stock only expensive free-market versions of the stuff they need to play Davy Crockett.

The second mandatory condition was that the families of certain named dissidents must be allowed to leave China, and it deserves a salute. A year of negotiation was required to accomplish this, and it is little enough, but we all should be grateful. A less serious achievement was the president's getting China to agree to a visit by a team of American technicians to talk about its jamming of Voice of America radio broadcasts.

About the other conditions there is not much to be said, because nothing much happened, at least nothing happened the way Clinton seemed to want it to. But three things did occur that are not irrelevant to American foreign policy and go to the point of some of the arguments in favor of extending China's most-favored-nation status.

First, China tried to ship chemicals for munitions to Iran (whether they got there or not, I can't say). Second, China sent technology for making missiles to Pakistan in violation of an international agreement. Third, China refused to cancel an underground nuclear test.

Now, place those three incidents alongside the argument that we have to "stay close" to the Chinese in order to influence them not to be a rogue dragon. We stayed as close as we could, and this is what (or some of what) they did. The underground nuclear test and the shipment to Pakistan are particularly revelatory. The stay-close arguers are especially concerned about North Korea. They want us to be insiders able to persuade China to persuade North Korea to cut it out; but despite the continuing trade status, nothing has come of that notion.

The Pakistan business has several sides to it, not the least interesting being the way Pakistan itself behaved. You will remember that Secretary of State Henry A. Kissinger and President Richard M. Nixon "tilted" toward Pakistan. That was realpolitik in the grand manner, like the posture proposed by the stay-close arguers. But our efforts to persuade Pakistan to lay off nuclear weapons have been no more successful than our appeals to China or North Korea.

There is, in fact, little evidence that staying close gives one nation any special influence over another. During the recent debate, Senator Bill Bradley gave a speech in which he called linking trade and human rights "old-think" characteristic of the Cold War and now mercifully behind us. The senator is mistaken. Actually we avoided linking human rights to anything during the Cold War, but we linked any bloody dictator to our bosom as long as he pretended to be anti-Communist.

In the present instance, because of President Clinton's "de-linking" human rights and most-favored-nation privileges, the Chinese are excellently positioned to do what they please. We have told ourselves that we need Chinese business. If we don't sell them airliners and electronic equipment, someone else will, and we will lose out in the competitive world market. If we don't buy their bicycles and T-shirts and kitchen utensils, we will have to pay more for them someplace that doesn't have such a repressive labor policy, and that will upset the great American shopper.

The Chinese have certainly heard what our business lobbyists have been saying. They have seen our government make a show of thinking about the issues and then cave in completely to the business demands. This does not surprise them. To the extent that they are still Communists, they expect our bourgeois government to be obedient to business interests.

And this should not surprise us, for we, too, believe that it's the economy, stupid, and only the economy. The nation and citizenship and human rights are subservient to questions of trade and finance. The argument for free trade assumes as much. Subscribing to that argument, we do not speak with authority when we suggest that it's not nice to beat people up and work them to death. The Chinese reasonably reply that there is no accounting for tastes.

As it happens, we have a shining example on the other side. For years we heard the same stay-close argument about South

Africa. An unorganized movement of students and writers and athletes and human rights activists gradually brought about the isolation of South Africa from civilized discourse. We could speak with authority because we proved willing to give up profitable business to make our point. It still required the combined efforts of Nelson Mandela and F. W. De Klerk, two truly great men of the twentieth century, to end apartheid, but even they scarcely could have done it without the moral stance of the civilized world.

On the record, the China card is more likely a joker than an ace.

[7/94]

Trickle-Down Greed

In a very short time neo-conservatism and neo-liberalism have gone a very long way toward destroying the morale of the American people. By "morale" I do not mean merely eagerness for life or sense of well-being, though these are included. More fundamental than psychological tone are morale as mores and morale as morality. It is these that are being destroyed. For the first time in the history of the world, a society is being deliberately and cheerily based on the proposition that it's good to be greedy. The world has certainly seen greedy people before, and many of these have been complacently sure of their right to their riches; but never before, I think, have the rich pretended that they benefit the poor by stealing from them.

For forty years—since the end of World War II—we have been giving ourselves quite a beating. It is an argument for our strength that we have survived McCarthyism and Vietnam and Watergate. Yet these traumata were not comparable to Reaganomics. Very few—certainly not including McCarthy himself—saw Red-baiting as more than a political ploy; tragic though Vietnam was, it cannot be seriously argued that we embarked on it to get anything for ourselves; Watergate was an ad hoc lunge for personal survival, not a way of life proposed for a society.

What is happening now is the corruption of the economic elite, that is to say the rich, who are assured that they will serve mankind better the richer they manage to become. This is not Adam Smith's "invisible hand" guiding entrepreneurs—that is, doers—for the public good. Our new rich are expected to work their miracles merely by being rich, not by doing anything at all. This doctrine is of course not without its recent forerunners, including the "maxi-tax" of 50 percent on earned income that produced, in 1972 and after, a rank and gross efflorescence of six- and seven-figure executive salaries. Then there is the flaccid side of consumerism, which, under the tutelage of television, presents living it up as the aim of life. And it says a great deal that for many years now men who think of themselves as honorable have used the term "tax shelter" without shame or even a trace of embarrassment.

For a parallel to our present debauch, one must go back to the Germany of World War I and its aftermath. The Junkers and industrialists made no pretense of uplifting their fellowmen, but their greediness provides a chilling example of how the morale of a society is destroyed *from the top*. It is often contended that the inflation of 1922–23—with its wheelbarrows of marks for a loaf of bread—ruined the middle class and so destroyed the society. Actually it was the other way around. The center did not hold because it had already been destroyed by the war.

Hjalmar Schacht, no wild-eyed radical in spite of his middle names (Horace Greeley), wrote of "the bountiful flow of money [during the war] from the coffers of the Treasury into the pockets of the producers [industrialists and Junker agriculturalists]" and contrasted this with the relatively heavy wartime taxation in Great Britain and the United States. After the war there was "the impression made on the public by the spectacle continually paraded before their eyes of particular undertakings and firms expanding their concerns, acquiring new works or erecting new buildings, amid the general monetary collapse, all with the aid of paper mark credits which they were able to obtain at will and repay in currency which every day was worth less and less. The private banks, in giving such paper mark credits, did so at the expense of their depositors or at the expense of the Reichsbank."

Change a few words, and you might think you were reading newspaper accounts of American oil companies, which insisted that they needed their windfall profits in order to drill for more oil but instead used them to start an office machines company (Exxon), buy Montgomery Ward (Mobil), and try to gobble up "competitors" (Mobil again). Or you may be reminded of Dupont borrowing $4 billion to buy Conoco, or of U.S. Steel, begging the government for protection against foreign competition, while using its credit not to update its obsolete plants, but to buy Marathon Oil.

In Germany, since the rich insisted on being rewarded rather than taxed, and since the middle class had, by 1922, already been despoiled, resort was finally had to the printing press. Speculation, as Schacht tells us, "spread to the smallest circles of the population."

I'm not saying that we are condemned in a Santayanaesque way to repeat this or any other history. I *am* saying that if you want to destroy an economy, the first thing to do is to corrupt the rich. The rot will spread very fast indeed, simply because the rich are the ones with the money.

Money is a sign of faith. The full faith and credit of some institution are behind it. Money is good if it is issued in good faith and credited—accepted—in good faith. The question of faith extends far beyond the relationship of the one who tenders the money and the one who accepts it. Tenderer and acceptor must have faith in each other, and they also must have faith in the relative stability of the economy and the relative equity of the society in which they participate. The acceptor must have faith that someone else will accept the money when he decides to spend it; and the tenderer must have faith that the society will be stable enough and equitable enough to allow him to enjoy what he bought with the money he tendered.

Money circulates only when these faiths are living. To the extent that these faiths are compromised, the money is compro-

The Morals of the Marketplace

Ethics was a big topic in 1987. This was the doing of Ivan Boesky, Michael Milken, Leona Helmsley, Bess Meyerson, Jim and Tammy Bakker, and a gap-toothed Marine lieutenant colonel, whose name I don't recall. Those cynics who consider Lucifer/ Satan the hero of *Paradise Lost* were not surprised, nor were those realists who observed that the remembered hero of Watergate is not John G. Sirica but G. Gordon Liddy.

In all the talk, business ethics came in for special attention, and many an editorial proposed required ethics courses in business schools. Lester C. Thurow, of MIT's Sloan School of Management, resisted the idea on the ground that the blight, if any, goes much too deep to be reached by a tacked-on series of lectures or bull sessions. Morals, he said, should have been learned at home and in the community long before graduate school. I resisted the special course idea, too, but on the ground that if students have been learning bad ethics or no ethics, it is because they have been taught bad economics.

Economics used to be called an ethical science, an expression that resonates oddly in our ears. Come to think of it, our term, "social science," gives off similar vibrations. Social relations surely have an ethical aspect (if there is such a thing as ethics), while the propositions of the natural sciences (which are what we think of as proper science) have no such aspect at all. There is nothing moral or immoral about the solar system, or about the way electrons bond, or even about AIDS. Morals may be—certainly are—involved in the transmission of AIDS, but the physiology of the disease is neither right nor wrong. Indeed, it is only because the disease is a natural phenomenon that there is any hope of controlling or curing it. Even the calls for sexual abstinence must depend on the fact that the disease obeys natural laws and is neither a random accident nor a supernatural visitation.

"Nature to be controlled," as Francis Bacon said, "must be obeyed." Thus disease control (which is a human end) uses medicines (which are natural means). Thus engineers use the principles of physics to achieve their ends. The ends are not natural, but the means are. It is often argued that economics presents a parallel situation. In 1874, Léon Walras, in his *Elements of Pure Economics*, distinguished at considerable length between economics as an ethical science, which considered what ought to be done; economics as an art, which taught how to do it; and economics as pure science, which described how it worked. Toward the end of the century, a similar tripartite analysis was made by John Neville Keynes (John Maynard's father). In our day, Milton Friedman, perhaps indulging a puckish humor, has quoted favorably from the senior Keynes's work.

The parallel between physiology or physics on the one hand and pure economics on the other is, however, false. There is no such thing as pure economics. Physiology and physics can be studied—must be studied—without regard to the willful act of any individual or group of individuals. But no such antiseptic event occurs in economics. Walras, whose work was hailed by Joseph Schumpeter as "the only work of an economist that will stand comparison with the achievements of theoretical physics," opened his analysis, after a long introduction, with the observation, "Value in exchange, when left to itself, arises spontaneously in the market as the result of competition." This pure proposition is, however, immediately corrupted by willful humanity: "As buyers, traders make their *demands* by *outbidding* each other. As sellers, traders make their *offers* by *underbidding* each other." (Walras's emphases.)

Without those traders with their demands and offers, there is no economics, pure or applied. But with those traders, economics becomes inextricably immersed in questions of morals. I do not mean merely that trade is impossible unless traders abjure fraud (at least up to a point), although certainly this is true. What I do mean is that demands and offers—the fundamental elements of "pure" economics—are not acts of God or events of nature but acts of human beings who necessarily define themselves by what they do, including what they do in the marketplace. Perhaps more to the point: Demands and offers can be understood only as acts of will.

There has been no lack of attempts to develop other explanations, which form the division of economics known as value theory. Prices are determined by the reconciliation of demands and offers, and demands and offers are said to be determined by values. There are three leading explanations of value. The first, found prominently in Adam Smith and Karl Marx, holds that things become valuable commodities in accordance with the amount of labor that goes into their production. The second, advanced by Jeremy Bentham, argues that only useful things are valuable, and that utility derives from the promotion of pleasure or the avoidance of pain. The third, credited by Léon Walras to his father, Auguste, founds value on *rareté*, which is a combination of utility and scarcity.

All these explanations turn out to have exceptions. The labor theory cannot explain why a house in the Houston suburbs that sold for a quarter of a million dollars only yesterday can be bought for half that price today and will sell for some different price tomorrow. The utility theory cannot explain why proprietary drugs are more expensive than their generic equivalents. The simple scarcity theory cannot explain why gem-quality diamonds are more expensive than bluebird nests. Put them all together in the *rareté* theory, and you still can't explain why base-ball stars are paid in the millions of dollars and croquet experts have to pay to enter tournaments.

Of course, the problem of the exceptions has not gone unnoticed. The typical solution turns on a relaxed definition of utility. Proprietary drugs, for example, may be said to be more useful to some people because they carry an implicit guarantee of quality and so enhance satisfaction and pleasure or suppress apprehension and pain. The greater perceived utility naturally results in a higher price.

But see what has happened. The utility theory, like all the theories, was introduced to provide an objective foundation to value. Bentham intended his "felicific calculus" to be the equivalent of Newton's laws of motion. But the foundation is actually highly subjective. Some people are pleased by drugs' brand names and some are pained by the higher prices. Bentham himself summed up the situation in an aphorism: "Quantity of pleasure being equal, pushpin is as good as poetry." One man's pleasure is another man's pain. Utility is what each individual says it is; it has none of the universality of gravity.

The consequence was, as it ironically happened, noted by William Stanley Jevons, a leader in developing Bentham's utilitarianism into the modern quasi-mathematical theory of marginal utility. Calling for increased efforts to collect economic statistics, he wrote, "The price of a commodity is the only test we have of the utility of the commodity to the purchaser. . . ." And, he might have added, of its utility to the seller, too. Price may be explained by utility, but all we know of utility is price.

The other value theories are no less circular. Marx recognizes that a lot of labor can go into producing positively harmful commodities; he therefore avers that the only labor that makes value is "socially useful" labor. Thus it is not labor that is the test of value; it is value that is the test of labor. The tree is known by his fruit. Walras's *rareté*, too, leans on the weak reed of utility, as well as on scarcity.

The only way to keep a circular argument from chasing its tail is not to let the chase get started. Let us, therefore, return to the men and women who did the price paying of Jevons, the offering and demanding of Walras, and the laboring and social evaluating of Marx. Who are these essential people? As Pogo might say, we have met them, and they are us.

The various value theories we have mentioned all try to make us into passive agents controlled by the economic counterpart of nature. Even perfect competition (the state imagined to provide perfect liberty) requires everyone to be what is called a price taker. Prices are then said to be made by the market. Those who quarrel with the idea of perfect competition tend to do so on the ground that competition never is and never has been perfect. That is true enough, but the reason for this is that the notion of an impersonal market that sets prices is a pathetic fallacy.

Farmers are the standard textbook examples of price takers, unable to influence the price of what they sell, whether they produce more or less, and whether they sell now, or later, or never. But if all producers and all consumers—that is, all human beings—are price takers, where do prices come from? Only cynics claim that the individual voter is insignificant because he or she is only one among tens of millions. The republic will not collapse if I fail to vote, but it will collapse if no one votes. It is the same with economic agents. Someone has to set a price, or there is no price system and no economics. An economy of passive agents is a contradiction in terms.

Economics is one of the modes of ethics. Pure economics—economics without people and lives without ethics—is a myth. Morality can't somehow be tacked onto economic affairs, which otherwise are amoral. Ethics is there at the beginning, or it is not there at all. It is always there because there is no economics that does not concern human acts, and all human acts are acts of will. What is true of economics, the theory of business enterprise, is obviously true of business itself. Business ethics is not merely the proposition that honesty is the best policy. The ethical question, in business and everywhere, is, What sort of person am I? There's no escaping it. That question is posed by everything I do.

[9/87]

Bishops Move Diagonally

I've been reading a fascinating document called *Economic Justice for All*. It is a pastoral "letter" (a small book, actually) approved by a vote of 225 to 9 by the National Conference of Catholic Bishops.

I hasten to put on the record that I am not now and never have been a member of the Catholic Church. I admit that, once upon a time when the world was young and I was twelve, I was received as a member by the State Street Congregational Church of Portland, Maine; and I recognize that there is a sense in which all of us in the Western world are Christians, just as we all are also Jews, Greeks, Romans, and Visigoths. But as to theology, it's been a long time since I was even agnostic.

So I approached the bishops' letter warily. I'd not have approached it at all if it hadn't been attacked by George Will, William E. Simon, and William F. Buckley, Jr. Anything hated by these people can't be all bad.

Well, it is, as I say, a fascinating document. Let me quote from it:

Quote: "Every economic decision and institution must be judged in light of whether it protects or undermines the dignity of the human person."

Quote: "All people have a right to participate in the economic life of society. . . . For it is through employment that most individuals and families meet their material needs, exercise their talents and have an opportunity to contribute to the larger community."

Quote: "We cannot separate what we believe from how we act in the marketplace and the broader community, for this is where we make our primary contribution to economic justice."

Quote: "In some industries the mobility of capital and technology makes wages the main variable in the cost of production. Overseas competitors with the same technology but with wage rates as low as one-tenth of ours put enormous pressure on U.S. firms to cut wages, relocate abroad or close. U.S. workers and their communities should not be expected to bear these burdens alone."

Quote: "The investment of human creativity and material resources in the production of weapons of war makes these economic problems even more difficult to solve."

Quote: "The common bond of humanity that links all persons is the source of our belief that the country can attain a renewed public moral vision."

Quote: "Minimum material resources are an absolute necessity for human life. If persons are to be recognized as members of the human community, then the community has an obligation to help fulfill these basic needs unless an absolute scarcity of resources makes this strictly impossible. No such scarcity exists in the United States today."

Quote: "Social justice implies that persons have an obligation to be active and productive participants in the life of society and that society has a duty to enable them to participate in this way."

Quote: "Work should enable the working person to become 'more a human being,' more capable of acting intelligently, freely and in ways that lead to self-realization."

Quote: "The concentration of privilege that exists today results far more from institutional relationships that distribute power and wealth inequitably than from differences in talent or lack of desire to work."

Quote: "Many in the lower middle class are barely getting by and fear becoming victims of economic forces over which they have no control."

Quote: "As individuals and as a nation we are called to make a fundamental 'option for the poor.' "

Quote: "The 'option for the poor' is not an adversarial slogan that pits one group or class against another. Rather it states that the deprivation and powerlessness of the poor wounds the whole community."

Quote: "Meeting fundamental human needs must come before the fulfillment of desires for luxury consumer goods, for profits not conducive to the common good and for unnecessary military hardware."

Quote: "Basic justice . . . recognizes the priority of policies and programs that support family life and enhance economic participation through employment and widespread ownership of property."

Quote: "The economy is not a machine that operates according to its own inexorable laws, and persons are not mere objects tossed about by economic forces."

Quote: "The task of creating a more just U.S. economy is the vocation of all and depends on strengthening the virtues of public service and responsible citizenship in personal life and on all levels of institutional life."

Quote: "The dignity of workers also requires adequate health care, security for old age or disability, unemployment compensation, healthful working conditions, weekly rest, periodic holidays for recreation and leisure, and reasonable security against arbitrary dismissal."

Quote: "We firmly oppose organized efforts, such as those now regrettably seen in this country, to break existing unions and prevent workers from organizing. Migrant agricultural workers today are particularly in need of the protection, including the right to organize and bargain collectively. U.S. labor law reform is needed to meet these problems as well as to provide more timely and effective remedies for unfair labor practices."

Quote: "It is unfair to expect unions to make concessions if managers and stockholders do not make at least equal sacrifices."

Quote: "Large corporations and large financial institutions have considerable power to help shape economic institutions within the United States and throughout the world. With this power goes responsibility and the need for those who manage it to be held to moral and institutional responsibility."

Quote: "Business and finance have the duty to be faithful trustees of the resources at their disposal. No one can ever own capital resources absolutely or control their use without regard for others and society as a whole."

Quote: "Resources created by human industry are also held in trust. Owners and managers have not created this capital on their own."

Quote: "Widespread distribution of property can help avoid excessive concentration of economic and political power. For these reasons ownership should be made possible for a broad sector of our population."

Quote: "Support of private ownership does not mean that anyone has the right to unlimited accumulation of wealth."

Quote: "Governments must provide regulations and a system of taxation which encourage firms to preserve the environment, employ disadvantaged workers, and create jobs in depressed areas. Managers and stockholders should not be torn between their responsibilities to their organizations and their responsibilities towards society as a whole."

Quote: "We must ask whether our nation will ever be able to modernize our economy and achieve full employment if we continue to devote so much of our financial and human resources to defense-related activities."

Quote: "The risk of inflationary pressures resulting from expansionary policies is very real. Our response to this risk, however, must not be to abandon the goal of full employment, but to develop effective policies that keep inflation under control."

Quote: "We recommend increased support for direct job creation programs targeted on the long-term unemployed and those with special needs."

Quote: "Across the nation, in every state and locality, there is ample evidence of social needs that are going unmet. Many of our parks and recreation facilities are in need of maintenance and repair. Many of the nation's bridges and highways are in disrepair. We have a desperate need for more low-income housing. Our educational systems, day care services, senior citizen services and other community programs need to be expanded. At the same time there are 8 million Americans looking for productive and useful work."

Quote: "The nation should renew its efforts to develop effective affirmative action policies that assist those who have been excluded by racial or sexual discrimination in the past."

Quote: "In comparison with other industrialized nations, the United States is among the more unequal in terms of income distribution. Moreover, the gap between rich and poor in our nation has increased during the last decade."

Quote: "We believe congress should raise the minimum wage in order to restore some of the purchasing power it has lost due to inflation."

Quote: "Efforts that enable the poor to participate in the ownership and control of economic resources are especially important."

Quote: "Diversity and richness in American society are lost as farm people leave the land and rural communities decay."

Quote: "We continue to support a progressive land tax on farm acreage to discourage the accumulation of excessively large holdings."

Quote: "We are dismayed that the United States, once the pioneer in foreign aid, is last among the 17 industrialized nations in the Organization for Economic Cooperation and Development in percentage of gross national product devoted to aid."

Quote: "Rather than promoting U.S. arms sales, especially to countries that cannot afford them, we should be campaigning for an international agreement to reduce this lethal trade."

Quote: "In our 1919 Program of Social Reconstruction we observed 'the full possibilities of increased production will not be realized as long as the majority of workers remain mere wage earners. The majority must somehow become owners, at least in part, of the instruments of production.' "

There is nothing in the passages I have quoted—and, aside from some theology, very little in the pastoral as a whole—that constant readers have not read in this space, perhaps somewhat less solemnly expressed. This is what disturbs me about the document. My instinctive response is to follow the Ben Hecht–like film writer in *Boy Meets Girl* who, when seconded in skulduggery by a pompous producer, snarls, "Stay off of our side, B. G."

Now, why do I respond in this way? Well, for one thing, the Catholic Church in America has a long record of association with illiberal causes. As prime recent examples, I think of the Legion of Decency (which tried to censor Faulkner, among others), the holding of federal aid to education for ransom (until outmaneuvered by President Lyndon Johnson), and the continuing worldwide opposition to birth control. Somehow, causes like these have been enthusiastically nurtured by the Church, while liberal causes, like the astonishing 1919 call for employee ownership, have tended to be stillborn.

Then there is the question of the separation of church and state. This issue has been raised for their purposes by Catholic laymen who disagree with the bishops. James J. Kilpatrick, writing for the Universal Press Syndicate, climaxes his diatribe with a citation (obligatory in such polemics) of Edmund Burke's *Reflections on the Revolution in France* and concludes with these ungracious reflections. "The bishops know the working of the marketplace by hearsay; they themselves, living well-fed and protected lives, are as innocent as kittens of economic risk and insecurity. When they involve the church in lobbying for changes at the World Bank and the IMF, all in the name of moral instruction, they trespass upon the boundary that wisely separates the pulpit from the political arena." Instinctively I find the argument of his final clause congenial. And yet—

And yet there is nothing in the First Amendment that forbids clergymen of whatever persuasion from speaking their minds on any matter whatever. (If you argue that churches that engage in politics should lose their tax exemptions, I counter that *all* churches should lose their tax exemptions.) Moreover, for years a standard charge against the Catholic Church in Latin America was that its silence on social questions in effect supported political and economic repression.

What is truly dangerous—what absolutely corrupts the democratic process—is one-issue politics, like the current right-to-life movement. *Economic Justice for All* is not a one-issue document. The public press has given it less attention than it deserves. I fear that the bishops' parishioners, too, have passed by on the other side.

[3/87]

No Concordance

I'm on a new mailing list, and I suppose you are, too. It calls itself the Concord Coalition, and it seems to be the plaything of former Senator Warren Rudman, Republican, of New Hampshire, and former Senator Paul Tsongas, Democrat, of Massachusetts.

If I didn't know anything about the two ex-senators and had to judge their organization solely by its mailing piece, I'd have difficulty in deciding whether they're extraordinarily stupid or extraordinarily slick. Either way, they're dangerous, and are likely to make the next few years less pleasant than we'd have found them otherwise.

Let's talk about the slickness first, because that's more fun. Their bag, as you know, is deficit reduction. In his "Dear Friend" letter to me, Mr. Rudman writes, underlined, *"Our goal is nothing short of changing public opinion to demand less, not more, deficit spending and force the elimination of the deficit."*

Now, if you read that quickly, you may get the idea that they're out to lobby the president and Congress to do something about the deficit. But that can't be their intention, for they ask me for a "special tax-deductible dues contribution," and so far as I know, you can't get a tax exemption for your organization if you plan to lobby the legislature. Common Cause doesn't have tax exemption, nor does the Council on Foreign Relations nor the National Association of Manufacturers nor the National Organization of Women nor the National Rifle Association nor the Academy of American Poets nor the American Automobile Association.

Some of the organizations on my little list play pretty hard ball, but most of them don't back candidates, and it's impossible to say with a straight face that the Concord Coalition is less "political" than they are. Either the Coalition is a couple of mighty slick lawyers, or they're encouraging violation of the law right off the bat. They are cute enough, however, to add in a postscript that "contributions are tax-deductible to the extent permitted by law." (Personal subscriptions to *The New Leader* are also tax-deductible "to the extent permitted by law," which, I regret to say, is not to any extent at all.)

And that's not the worst of it. The bookkeeping reason for the deficit is that our expenditures are too high and our taxes are too low. The Coalition proposes that tax collections be reduced by the amounts otherwise payable on the contributions they receive. By their very existence they're increasing the deficit they complain about. If that isn't cynicism, what is it?

It may be stupidity.

But I doubt it. Both Mr. Rudman and Mr. Tsongas are grown men, and they're both (I think) lawyers. They've both spent a lot of time thinking about taxes, and presumably they both can add and subtract.

Mr. Rudman also makes a point of the fact that "the hundreds of hours that Paul and I are putting into The Concord Coalition are strictly on a volunteer basis." Not to worry. They're both entitled (I think that's the word) to comfortable government pensions, complete with cost-of-living adjustments (a.k.a. COLAs), not to mention better health insurance than you'll ever see. Besides, if theirs is a truly tax-exempt organization, their expenses of running hither and yon to appear on talk shows are deductible. But not otherwise, although the expenses might be legitimate charges against whatever contributions they manage to collect.

Well, that's all good for a chuckle or two in this winter of our discontent. But what will happen to the economy if the Concord Coalition gets its way won't be funny. And given the results of the recent election, it would be inadvisable to bet they won't succeed without even trying.

So let's look at the deficit. The estimate for 1995 (the fiscal year that started the first of last October) is $176.1 billion. That's down substantially from the $220.1 billion deficit of FY 1994. In relation to GDP, it's the smallest deficit we've had since 1979. But it's still a lot of money. Suppose that, by constitutional amendment or otherwise, that deficit could be wiped out. What would become of all that money?

Would you and I get refunds for our share of it? Or would the government deposit it where it could earn interest in a Texas savings and loan (if any survives)? Or would it be stashed away in Fort Knox? Or could we use it to pay off our trading debts to the Germans and the Japanese? Or to buy back the bonds they've bought from us? Or would it be an advance payment on the following year's budget?

The correct answer, of course, is: None of the above. And the reason for that answer is that all those billions would not exist. They would not disappear, because they would never have existed. Not only would the money not exist, the goods and services the money was budgeted to buy would not exist, either.

Maybe you and I didn't want those goods and services, anyhow. Maybe we thought it was wasteful to spend money on them. Even so, we'd better stop a minute to consider what their nonexistence would mean to us, that is, to the economy.

First off, we can't cut government expenditures by $176.1 billion without firing people. And they won't all be lazy, faceless bureaucrats, because the federal government is not only the nation's largest employer, it's also the nation's largest purchaser of stuff produced by the private sector. (Where did you think the paper for the paperwork comes from?)

The point is that the people who will lose their jobs are fellow citizens; so when we talk about the number of them, we should never forget that they're ordinary people like you and me. The number is very large. I estimate it at 4,776,933, which I arrive at in this way: (1) The way the pie is cut in our economy today, labor gets about three-fifths of it, and three-fifths of $176.1 billion is $106.86 billion. (2) The average wage of workers in the United States is $22,370. (3) Divide (1) by (2) and you get 4,776,933 new recruits for the army of the unemployed.

That should push our unemployment well over ten million. In fact, when you consider the lost purchasing power of those four and three-quarter million people, and the lost business of the people who used to sell to them, there's little doubt that trimming $176.1 billion from the federal budget should enable us to set a new post-Depression high to our unemployment record, not to mention a new record for relief expenses.

I know, of course, the answer Messrs. Rudman and Tsongas would make to the foregoing, because I've heard Newt Gingrich touting a balanced-budget amendment, which would codify the problem. They'd say that cutting $176.1 billion out of the federal budget would so stimulate the private sector, overjoyed to get all that government off its back, that it would forget it had ever coined the word "downsizing" and would invest and expand its businesses to take up the slack and then some.

I'd not be surprised if the private sector talked that way; but I'd be astonished if it acted that way, because when businesspeople forget about politics and mind their businesses, they're not quite so stupid as they sometimes sound. If they're not investing and expanding now, there'd be no reason for them to do so if the deficit's cut. Taxes won't be a reason; the deficit is caused because taxes don't cover expenditures now. Budget balancing won't be accomplished by lightening up that side of the scales. Besides, the only taxes likely to be cut are capital-gains taxes, which will be dandy for speculators but will do nothing good for producing entrepreneurs and will probably increase the interest they have to pay. (I forgot: There's likely to be an attempt to get a cut for the middle class, too, meaning people with adjusted gross incomes up to $200,000.)

No, I think we can expect downsizing to continue, no matter what's done with the budget.

As constant readers know, I'm a mild-mannered chap; so I find it difficult to believe that the Concord Coalition is just another Trojan Horse. If they're really naive instead of slick or stupid, their naïveté goes pretty deep into their misunderstanding of economics. They don't begin to understand money and its role in the capitalist system.

They've possibly never wondered where the Federal Reserve notes in their pockets came from and what makes them worth more than the paper they're printed on. They've possibly never looked closely at a dollar bill. It says right on its face, "This note is legal tender for all debts, public and private." What does that mean? It means that it was issued by the government in payment for some good or service, and that, in the end, the government will take it back in payment of some fee or tax. In the meantime, the government owes a dollar to whoever holds the note. It is an acknowledgment of debt.

In the capitalist system, not all debt is money, but all money is debt. If the Concord Coalition gets rid of the $176.1 billion deficit, that much of the money supply will be washed out. Now, if business is to continue merely at its present sluggish pace, the $176.1 billion will have to be replaced from somewhere. Since it seems unlikely that private business will kick its downsizing habit any time soon (why should it, with GATT on the horizon?), state and local governments will have to pick up the slack and go deeper into debt to the tune of $176.1 billion. Needless to say, slumping federal services will force them to do some of that, anyhow. Deficit reduction turns out to be a scam shifting some federal burdens to the states, probably (I regretfully suspect) in the expectation that the burdens will be either fumbled or financed with a regressive sales tax.

As you will no doubt remember from "In Pursuit of a Fiscal Fantasy," the government can be in debt forever and ever, issu-

ing new bonds to pay off those that come due. All it has to be
able to do is to pay interest on the loans, and that would be no
problem at all if the Federal Reserve Board were at least moderately committed to the national welfare. AT&T and most of the
Fortune-500 companies and indeed almost all companies of
every size are constantly rolling over their debt in the same way.
Capitalism is a system based on borrowing and lending.

You and I could do the same if we were immortal. As it is, we
don't hesitate to go into debt to provide our family with a better
place to live and to give our children the best education possible.
Would we have done our children a favor if we hadn't made the
commitment, even though some of the debt may still be unpaid
at our death?

On reflection, I fear I must conclude that the Concord Coalition is not only slick but stupid.

[11/94]

The Reserve Takes Flight Once Again

On July 20, 1993, Federal Reserve Board chairman Alan Greenspan announced a fundamental change in the way the august body he heads looks upon the economy. This is not merely a tactical shift, as from easy money to tight money—although the Board's volatility on the tactical level is bad enough—but a basic rethinking of how the economy works and what the Board should therefore do. It is the second such revision in Greenspan's six and a half years as chairman, and the fourth in something under fourteen years. So many radical rethinkings in so few years suggest an unseemly flightiness in an institution whose primary excuse for existence is to provide financial stability beyond the turmoil of partisan politics.

Let's look at the record. On October 6, 1979, Paul A. Volcker, the then new chairman, revealed that thereafter the Reserve would "be placing greater emphasis on day-to-day operations of the supply of bank reserves, and less emphasis on confining short term fluctuation in the Federal rate" (the rate at which banks borrow reserves from each other overnight or for a day or two). Monetarism had taken charge.

For the next six or seven years we heard a great deal about M1 and its velocity. (In case you've forgotten, M1 is cash and traveler's checks and checking deposits; M2 is all that plus most savings accounts, money-market funds, and other odds and ends.) Milton Friedman, the leading monetarist, wanted M1 to grow annually between 3 and 5 percent. Expansion beyond 5 percent, he claimed, would cause inflation—instantaneously if the expansion was anticipated, or with a lag of a year if it was not. Not only that, but the inflation would accelerate without limit.

By 1986, expansion beyond 5 percent was surely anticipated by all rational economic agents, because it had not been below 5 percent for ten years. Yet in 1986, when M1 jumped 16.8 percent (and M2 jumped 9.4 percent), the Consumer Price Index rose only 1.9 percent—its smallest rise in twenty-two years. Monetarism clearly missed the call, and missed badly.

The Federal Reserve Board was left without a theory—that is, without a coherent idea of what it was doing or why. For the rest of Volcker's term, the nation was forced to rely on seat-of-the-pants judgments of officials whose cerebral judgments had proved sensationally wrongheaded.

In the spring of 1987, Alan Greenspan succeeded to the chairmanship and at once set three economists to work on an equation intended to use M2 to prophesy the price level two or more years ahead. Also, true to the teachings of Ayn Rand, he cut expansion of M1 and M2 back below the 5 percent target. And what did the CPI do? It surged ahead 4.4 percent in both 1987 and 1988.

Nevertheless, on June 13, 1989, the Reserve went to extraordinary lengths to publicize an equation that two years of labor by those three economists had produced. Well, the Reserve seems at last to have abandoned this equation, or the M2 theory behind it, which, Greenspan said last month, "has been downgraded as a reliable indicator."

Of course, the money supply never was a reliable indicator, for the simple reason that no one can say what it is. The Federal Reserve owlishly publishes aggregates it calls M1, M2, M3, and L. L is about six times M1. Friedman once said the number used did not matter, so long as one stayed with it. Since the tracks of the different aggregates have been substantially different, it would appear to have made some difference.

You would think that by this time we might all agree to stop fretting over the money supply. Yet the Reserve, perhaps for ritualistic reasons, has adopted a new target for M2 growth (1–5 percent), even though it acknowledges that hitting (or missing) the target won't indicate anything special.

The downgrading of M2 does not mean the chairman is without any indicator. He has mentioned only one aspect of his new one (and that I will discuss presently), but he has used it with results that can hardly be called encouraging. In his July 20 testimony before Congress, he forecast a second-quarter growth rate of 2.5–3.0 percent. Nine days later, the official number proved to be 1.6 percent.

I think I can promise you that the new indicator will continue to get things wrong. According to Greenspan, "one important guidepost" of the new indicator will be the so-called real interest rate: the actual rate minus the rate of inflation. When, as now, the federal-funds rate is about 3 percent and the CPI rate is about 3.5 percent, the "real" federal-funds rate is negative 0.5 percent. Anyone lending $1,000 at 3 percent gets back $1,030 at the end of a year, but his purchasing power will have shrunk to $993.95. So why should he lend? Because if he buries his money like the slothful servant in the Parable of the Talents, he will still have his $1,000 but his purchasing power will shrink to $965.

Greenspan thinks that's unfair and hints about raising the federal rate one-half a percentage point or more to make things even. Naturally, if he raises the federal rate, he effectively raises others, including those that are far from negative.

What Greenspan is threatening is a cost-of-living adjustment (COLA) for bankers. It is well understood by bankers and economists that COLAs on workers' wages are inflationary and should be resisted. How are Bankers' COLAs different? In a word, they aren't, and they cost the economy (that is, you and me) about $500 billion a year.

Although bankers do most of the talking about the interest

mised. This is true even of so-called hard currencies. Gold is pre-ferred to paper only by someone who wishes to opt out of the economy; but even such a person must have faith that some where and some when there will be an end to whatever prompts his preference for gold, and that someone else will then accept the gold in the ordinary course of living. If no such use for gold can be foreseen, if the hand of every man is indeed against every man, only guns and butter are worth accumulating. The Inca's hoard did him no good.

People fear that too much money will be issued unless it is tied to something tangible, like gold. But there is too much money in an economy only when a society's morale is sagging. The government can exhibit bad faith by taxing inequitably. The banks can exhibit bad faith by creating money for specula-tive rather than productive purposes. Both of these exhibitions are very visible today. The Federal Reserve Board may try its ut-most to fine-tune the economy, but it has not strength or means to overcome the effects of the bad faith except by destroying faith in the economy altogether. This is the notorious trade-off be-tween continuing inflation and deepening depression. Every ed-itorial writer in the land fears that if the Reserve releases its brakes on the money supply, the economy will, as they say, over-heat and inflation will, as they say, roar out of control. But these bitter alternatives are inexorable only where a people's morale has been destroyed, where the rich are rewarded rather than taxed, where greed is held to be the height of virtue.

[1/82]

rate, their role in lending is comparatively passive. If no one wants to produce a better mousetrap or buy a better automobile or take a flier in the stock market, bankers must sit on their money. Putting consumers and speculators aside for the moment, consider a company with plans for a better mousetrap, requiring investment in a factory, equipping it with machinery, buying supplies, hiring workers. In 1993, the company figured all that to cost $10 million. For convenience, let's say it could borrow at prime, then 6 percent, for an annual interest expense of $600,000. It felt it could just about swing it.

But Greenspan has given bankers a 1.5 percentage point COLA. At 1.5 percent, the interest expense is up to $750,000 — an increase of 25 percent in cost, or a decrease of 25 percent in the amount of money the mousetrap company can afford to borrow.

The company then has three options: (1) Abandon or scale down the expansion and the jobs it would have created. (2) Raise prices to cover the added cost. (3) Make do with lower profits, which would make future borrowing still more expensive. These options are faced every day by every company, large or small. Even rich companies that do not need to borrow must consider the opportunity cost of using their own money instead of lending it out.

If investment is as important as everyone says it is, and if stable prices are as important as the Reserve says they are, Greenspan's 1.5-point adjustment would be bad for every company and for the whole economy in one of the ways I've noted, and quite possibly in all three ways. Not only that, but the bond market would fall, as it necessarily does when interest rates rise. The stock market would surely follow after, for the same reason — and, considering its present fragile highs, could very well crash.

The interest rate, not the money supply, is what the Federal Reserve Board can control directly and assuredly. It sets the federal-funds rate and the discount rate, and it controls them by buying or selling Treasury bonds on the open market. In order to buy, it offers a high price, which is the same as a low interest rate. The banks that sell bonds thus increase their cash reserves, putting additional downward pressure on the interest rate.

If all this activity increases borrowing, as it is likely to do, it will increase the money supply, because money is negotiable debt. But who cares? It is the interest rate that matters to the economy, and it is through stabilizing the rate at a low level (less than half what it is today) that the Reserve could (if it would) do its bit to stabilize the economy.

Milton Friedman has long contended that the Federal Reserve Board has used its great powers so erratically in the past that it should be put under strict statutory regulation. He may be right. But he would regulate the growth of the money supply within a narrow range, even though he doesn't know what the money supply is, and the Board has shown it doesn't know how to control it, whatever it is.

That there is a determinate money supply, and that its size determines the price level, is an old mercantilist idea. It was valid enough when money was something rare and tangible and not readily reproducible, like gold or silver. The capitalist system turns on borrowing, however, and borrowing depends on the interest rate, and the lower the rate the greater the economy. How long must we allow ourselves to be deluded by archaic ideas?

[8/93]

The Oktoberfest of 1987

One listens with astonishment to the explanations of the Great Crash of 1987. With unprecedented unanimity, pundits and brokers and bankers and public officials blame the budget deficit and the foreign trade deficit.

In his October 22 press conference, President Reagan seemed not to understand. He was being pushed into what the press called a summit conference with congressional leaders to see about reducing the budget deficit, but his heart plainly wasn't in it. Look, he protested, the budget has been Gramm-Rudmanning down and will go down some more, even without a conference. He couldn't see what's so bad about that trend, although he was ready to blame the Democrats for anything anyone happened to think bad about it.

It's not hard to share his bewilderment. If the budget deficit is a problem, it is in fact being reduced. A few hard-liners may be upset that the reductions are not greater and faster; yet most people (including the president) have absorbed enough from Keynes (whom the president gracelessly and ignorantly disparaged) to know that doing too much too fast with the deficit would be a pretty sure prescription for a recession. Keynes himself might well have thought the reductions an utter mistake at this time. But he is dead (as we all are in the long run), and what is actually being done is what the pundits say Wall Street wants. If Wall Street is really upset by the deficit, it should have broken two years ago, when the deficit was higher, or five years ago, when the deficits (and the market itself) started their dramatic climb.

No, the deficit story is a fairy tale. It is implausible on its face, and its implausibility can readily be tested. We had a pretty good market crash in 1929. What caused that? Well, one thing is certain: The 1929 crash wasn't caused by a budget deficit, for the budget was in surplus that year to the tune of $700 million, which was a lot of money back then. Either the crashes of 1929 and 1987 are totally different breeds of animal, or deficits had nothing to do with them.

The two crashes did, nevertheless, have one thing in common. Both were preceded by prolonged and steep run-ups of the stock markets. That's no surprise: You have to have attained a certain height to be able to make an attention-getting fall. What signifies is that both climbs were speculative—business didn't improve all that much. Though in both years all persons of prominence assured us that the economy was fundamentally sound (there seem to be no other words to express this meaningless thought), there was not in either year a justification for the heights the market reached.

Speculation, however, doesn't need a justification; it merely needs an occasion. The necessary occasion is a very simple one: Some people have to have more money than they know what to do with. Literally.

We have been satisfying this requirement. As the recently announced figures from the Census Bureau show, the number of people with large incomes has increased in the decade and a half from Nixon through Reagan. The top 20 percent of American families had an average income of $126,415 last year and together engrossed 46.1 percent of all personal income. More important, they have improved and are improving their position at the expense of both the middle class and the poor.

Now, it is practically impossible to spend a million a year on living well, and it is perfectly possible to be pretty comfortable, even in a high-priced city like New York, on as little as a hundred thousand. You can, of course, spend pots of money collecting lead soldiers or used postage stamps or post-impressionist masters. The trouble with such collections is that, even at a moderate rate of inflation, they increase in value very rapidly and so add to rather than deplete your wealth. So lots of people have lots of money.

The supply-side theory, to which Reagan pledged continued devotion the other night, contemplates that the rich, thwarted in their struggle to consume their income, will invest it. But when 20 percent or more of the economy's productive capacity is lying unused, the possibilities of prudent new investment are severely limited. What to do? Nothing for it but to take a flier in the market. At the same time, the rich of the rest of the world have the same problem—and the same solution. On top of all this are the mutual funds, the pension plans, the educational and charitable endowments, the insurance reserves, and the unabashed speculations—all of which add up to a lot of money chasing a limited number of shares of stock.

Ingenious men have worked very hard to increase the number and kinds of pieces of paper to buy and sell. Two ways have especially recommended themselves: the development of the stock futures markets, and the computerization of Wall Street. The first created new products (as the brokers call them) out of nothing but the eagerness to speculate; the second, by enabling an increased velocity of trading, increased the opportunities to speculate, just as an increase in the velocity of money in effect increases the money supply.

There was also a partially contrary movement. Takeovers and buyouts, which generally substituted debt for equity, reduced the number of shares of some stocks available for speculation and at the same time greatly enhanced the taste for speculating.

The most elementary fact about a bull market is that it absolutely and unceasingly depends on sucking more money into it.

If there are 100 shares of stock, and $100 available for investment, the price of each share will fluctuate narrowly around a dollar, no matter what incantations are uttered by market analysts and government officials. If the number of available shares is reduced, or the number of available dollars increased, the price will rise proportionately. But all who anticipate a further increase in available funds will become more eager in their bids, in the expectation of quickly and profitably selling what they buy to the holders of the new money. Thus Holland's Tulipmania was sustained, and thus the Great Bull Market of the twenties, and thus the Reagan-Thatcher-Nakasone market that's now crashed.

Since one way or another the number of pieces of paper to speculate in has greatly increased, the number of dollars to sustain the recent bull market had to be increased even more greatly, and this has been done in two ways: the shift of trust and endowment funds out of the bond market and into the stock market, and the supply-side tax cuts for the wealthy. The former was substantially effected a couple of years ago, and the latter has gone about as far as it can go with the new tax law's reduction of the top rate to 28 percent. There's still a fantastic amount of money around, but it is no longer being increased rapidly.

The trade deficit is said to have joined with the budget deficit in scaring foreigners out of our market. This explanation of the crash overlooks what is ordinarily insisted on: the global interdependence of financial markets. It wasn't just Wall Street that laid an egg. Eggs were laid in Tokyo and Hong Kong and Sydney and London before the New York market opened on Black Monday. You might say that all over the world bull markets that had known no boundaries were suddenly fenced in.

Just as the reason for the crash is grievously misunderstood, so the policies proposed for dealing with it are grievously misconceived. Since what happened was caused by a substantial number of people having more money than they knew what to do with, it follows that it is counterproductive to resist taxing some of that money and applying it to public purposes, not excluding deficit reduction. The supply-side tax cuts were a disaster. Since the wealthy couldn't find enough new productive investments for their surplus funds, it follows that there hasn't been enough effectual demand (as Adam Smith would have said) to keep our existing productive capacity busy; so the enthusiasm devoted to union busting, entitlement shaving, welfare restricting, and real-wage reducing has been disastrously misdirected.

Our pundits seem able to behold the mote in German and Japanese eyes but not to consider the beam that is in ours. If the world economy would be strengthened by increased consumption in those lands (and it would), it can scarcely make sense to decrease consumption in ours. Over the past fifteen years the income share of the poorest 20 percent of our families—those who have to spend their incomes—has fallen 10.8 percent. An economy that reduces its aggregate demand in that way—and seems determined to do more—is not fundamentally sound.

[11/87]

Schumpeter Revisited

In preparation for a previous column I reread the passages I had underlined long ago in Joseph A. Schumpeter's *Capitalism, Socialism and Democracy*, a book whose first edition was published in 1942. The second edition appeared five years later, and the third in 1950. My copy is from the twenty-second printing of the paperback edition. All that adds up to sales in six figures.

It is a curious book. Its display of scholarship is casual and impressive. It contains less economics than history and what the Europeans call sociology (a more humane discipline than ours). Its style is informal, worldly-wise, and generally good natured, though a bitterness lurks behind several references to John Maynard Keynes and comes forward harshly in criticism of Schumpeter's Harvard colleague, Alvin H. Hansen, who is often meant but never named. (Hansen was a leading expositor of Keynes in America, and many now say he got it all wrong, but his possible mistakes about Keynes are not what bother Schumpeter.)

I don't propose to review either the work or the author's academic infighting. The book does, however, advance three propositions on which I should like to hang a tale or two. Number one comes at the opening of Part II: "Can capitalism survive? No, I do not think it can." Number two is at the opening of

Part III: "Can socialism work? Of course it can." These propositions don't look particularly plausible today, and they are not
helped by Schumpeter's reiterated disclaimer that he is not talking about the then-immediate future, but about a fifty-year trend
that has now run.

The third Schumpeter proposition is never explicitly stated
but is a two-part assumption, or definition, that underlies his
whole argument. The first part of the assumption is that economics, and capitalism in particular, is about the production of
physical things. The second part is that physical things are produced most abundantly when entrepreneurs are allowed or encouraged to compensate themselves at the rates roughly prevail-
ing before the First World War. Taking account also of
Schumpeter's notions about the family, it might not be too ex-
treme to say that the world he celebrates, and whose pasing he
foresees, is the world of Thomas Mann's *Buddenbrooks*.

That world has indeed passed; yet capitalism is today the sur-
vivor in its struggle with socialism. It has not, to be sure, survived
unchanged. It used to be said that America's Norman Thomas
brand of socialism never came close to succeeding at the polls
because the Democrats, and sometimes the Republicans, stole
its best ideas. (Thomas himself once told me he thought many
thousands of his votes simply weren't counted.) But that's not
what I have in mind.

I refer instead to a change in the meaning of private property,
surely a central concept in capitalism and in economics generally. In the United States the change as a matter of law was accomplished when the minority in an 1872 Supreme Court case
became the majority in another case some eighteen years later,
or just over a century ago.

The first instance was the Slaughter House Cases, in which
the minority argued that the state of Louisiana had deprived
New Orleans butchers of their property without due process of
law by requiring them to use a subsidized slaughterhouse at high
fixed fees. The majority upheld the state, relying on the com-
mon-law definition of property as physical things held exclu-

sively for one's own use. Since the butchers still had their shops and hooks and cleavers, they were not deprived of their property, even though the high fees made pursuit of their calling impracticable. The minority contended that property necessarily included its exchange value, or the right to use it for economic gain. Their definition of property began to appear in other state and federal courts, and finally prevailed in the first Minnesota Rate Case of 1890.

The story is elegantly told in John R. Commons's *The Legal Foundations of Capitalism*, a truly great book I've had occasion to mention several times in the past. As Commons points out, there is nothing in the common law or in the Constitution to support the new view. But Adam Smith could be cited on the primacy of labor and on the distinction between use value and exchange value; and *The Wealth of Nations* already had an odor of sanctity about it. More important, business practice was coming to depend almost exclusively on exchange value. Property was no longer a datum—merely a thing. It became an idea— what you could do with it to make money.

This fundamental shift in the meaning of property was a historical turning in the development of modern capitalism—and Schumpeter missed it, or missed most of it. For when property became an idea, production, too, became an idea. What distinguishes an idea is criticism. In fact, an idea demands criticism, for one idea thus leads to another. A mere thing, in contrast, is like Popeye: It is what it is. The point here is that a hundred years ago the meaning of property in the United States changed to embrace exchange value, and that correspondingly not only the economic meaning of production changed but the function of entrepreneurship as well.

Schumpeter's entrepreneur became obsolete, as he himself saw to some extent. "The entrepreneurial function," he wrote, "does not essentially consist in inventing anything or otherwise creating the conditions which the enterprise exploits. It consists in getting things done." Increasingly, Schumpeter continued, "technological progress is . . . becoming the business of trained

specialists who turn out what is needed and make it work in pre-
dictable ways. . . . Bureau and committee work tends to replace
individual action."

That is true enough. What Schumpeter does not see, however, is that a collegial enterprise can be a far more fulfilling
place to work and a far more responsible producer for the com-
monweal than anything built around his quasi-military entrepreneur. It ain't necessarily so, but it can be so.

The second Schumpeter assumption concerns the distribution of wealth and income, or who gets what and why. The last
chapter of his book is an address he delivered to the American
Economic Association ten days before his death on January 8,
1950. In it he said, "Capitalism does not merely mean that the
housewife may influence production by her choice between
peas and beans; or that the youngster may choose whether he
wants to work in a factory or on a farm; or that plant managers
have some voice in deciding what and how to produce: It means
a scheme of values, an attitude toward life, a civilization—the
civilization of inequality and of the family fortune." Well, he
doesn't mince words, does he?

Three years earlier, in the second edition of his book, Schumpeter made a forecast of the likely state of the economy in 1950.
As was only prudent, he protected his forecast with many provi-
sos, the chief of which were that 1950 would be a peak year in the
business cycle, and that New Deal (by then, Fair Deal) interfer-
ence with business (especially price controls and labor legisla-
tion) could be curtailed. As it turned out, the second proviso was
satisfied, but not the first; and he was right on the mark with one
of his predictions, but far off the mark with two others.

The accurate forecast was more demographics than economics: He expected the 1950 labor force to be "something like 61
million," and the currently accepted figure is 60.8 million. But
concerning that force (and now we're back in economics), he
wrote, "I do not see that the number of *statistically* unemployed
men and women can possibly be, in that year, below five or six
million. . . ." Relying on similar statistics, we find the actual

unemployment total to have been 3.3 million. Schumpeter went on to say, "On an average of good and bad years (statistical) unemployment should be higher than 5 or 6 million—7 to 8 perhaps." In fact, we didn't hit 8 million until thirty years later, in 1981, when the labor force was over 110 million, though we grazed it in 1975, when the labor force was 95 million.

Schumpeter's forecast of the GNP was way off in the other direction: $200 billion in 1928 dollars, as opposed to the actual $153 billion. One would, of course, expect lower unemployment to result in higher GNP, but we have a contrary picture. Can we account for the contrariness?

The key is the distribution of income. Schumpeter points out that, after a disgraceful period ending around the middle of the nineteenth century, the condition of the masses steadily improved. After all, capitalism is a mass-production system, while elite families' consumption goods are custom-made. "The capitalist achievement," he writes, "does not typically consist in providing more silk stockings for queens but in bringing them within the reach of factory girls in return for steadily decreasing amounts of effort." The problem, though, is that the proportionate shares of the national income remained essentially the same—as Schumpeter insisted they ought to.

Capitalist industry is far more productive and efficient than Schumpeter gave it credit for. Whether run by swashbuckling entrepreneurs or by committees of colorless technicians, industry can turn out the stuff. The question is, Who will buy?

Certainly his 7 or 8 million unemployed (then about a fifth of all wage earners) on the dole wouldn't be much of a market. Nor would the next three quintiles, whose income would be low because (according to the theory) their contribution would be low. The contribution of the entrepreneurs would be very great, but their numbers would be very small and, besides, they would not be substantial consumers of mass-produced goods. That leaves those just below the elite—say about a fifth of the population—as the only full-scale market for all of industry.

When you take Schumpeter's figures apart and scrutinize them, you can see why his projected GNP was so far off. The stuff wasn't turned out because there weren't enough buyers with enough money. The actual unemployment figures were much better than his estimates, but the distribution of income was not much better, and it is not much better today.

In the world of economic models, it doesn't matter whether the supply side or the demand side stimulates the economy. But in the real world of existing industry capable of high production, effectual demand (Adam Smith's phrase) is primary. Schumpeter's vision of a prosperous world led by entrepreneurial families never came to pass, because too many had little or no share in the prosperity. There was no justice in the shares, and no sound economics, either.

[4/92]

The Affluent Society Twenty-five
Years Later

The Affluent Society by John Kenneth Galbraith was published twenty-five years ago. Galbraith is one of the great economists of our time, and this is one of several great books he has published. It changed our way of looking at things. Even those who affect to sneer at the author for being funny must take it seriously. Attempts to dispute its thesis, such as F. A. Hayek's essay "The *Non Sequitur* of the 'Dependence Effect,' " end by missing the point.

Galbraith's attack on what he calls the conventional wisdom (he invented the term) moves against its unquestioning acceptance of two propositions: (1) that production is *per se* desirable, and (2) that consumer choices, through the market, guide production into channels that society values. The first proposition leads to the current worship of the GNP, some of whose absurdities I mentioned in this space last month. The exposure of the failure of the second proposition, *in an affluent society*, is the great contribution of Galbraith's book. He writes that "our concern for goods . . . does not arise in spontaneous consumer need. Rather, . . . it grows out of the process of production itself. If production is to increase, the wants must be effectively contrived. In the absence of contrivance, the increase would not occur. This is not true of all goods, but that it is true of a substantial part is sufficient."

It is sufficient for his argument, because if advertising or other contrivance has any effect at all, it must increase demand at the margin. And "since the demand for this part [of production] would not exist, were it not contrived, its utility or urgency, *ex* contrivance, is zero." Hence "the marginal utility of present aggregate output, *ex* advertising and salesmanship, is zero." From this it follows that private production is not sacrosanct, and it becomes possible to consider the likelihood that a clean environment may be more valuable than a newly packaged detergent.

In his attempted rebuttal, Hayek grants that "the tastes of man, as is true of his opinions and beliefs and indeed of his personality, are shaped in great measure by his cultural environment." This is not exactly Galbraith's point, but on the basis of it, Hayek finds it impossible to judge some tastes less urgent than others, though he himself puts great store by "the novels of Jane Austen or Anthony Trollope or C. P. Snow." Thus he undercuts his own position. If there is no way of judging relative wants, then there can be no way of judging the success of the economy in satisfying those wants, nor can there be any way of making things either better or worse. Economics becomes a waste of time, as much of what passes for economics certainly is.

Though many are uneasily aware that *The Affluent Society* is a book on morals, it is infrequently noted that it is a history book. For these reasons, those who think that economics is an immutable science of unchanging laws have trouble with it. Galbraith observes, for example, that "bad kings in a poorer world showed themselves quite capable, in their rapacity, of destroying or damaging the production of private goods by destroying the people and the capital that produced them." In such a world, laissez-faire was a reasonable response. But as Galbraith shows, what was reasonable then is not reasonable now. The world moves.

The world continues to move, and as a result one of the minor or incidental arguments of *The Affluent Society* has been super-

seded. It is not central to the main argument, but is a recommen-
dation of a particular strategy for practical politics.

Galbraith contends that many measures for the public good
are lost because liberals insist on raising "the essentially un-
related issue of equality." In the ensuing debate over progressive
vs. regressive taxation, a coalition of conservatives and simon-
pure liberals defeats the socially desirable program. As Voltaire
said, the best is the enemy of the good. Galbraith therefore urges
liberals to get on with the programs and live to fight another day
on the equality question.

Whether deliberately or not, the Democrats did in effect follow Galbraith's strategy in 1981. The Republicans were encouraged, even outbid, in "reforming" the tax laws to their liking.
Did they then acquiesce in the expansion of national programs
for the public good? Not that anyone noticed. The sight of blood
drove them mad. Even Stockman was shocked at their greed. It
would appear that at some times and with some people a civilized accommodation is impossible.

A convenient and scary summary of what has happened to the
tax laws is given in a short book or long pamphlet entitled
Inequity and Decline, by Robert S. McIntyre and Dean S. Tipps
of Citizens for Tax Justice. One of the virtues of this booklet is
that it shows that what happened in 1981 was not an isolated
event but had a history stretching back to the Nixon years and in
many respects earlier. Especially illuminating is the analysis of
the tax "revolt" that broke out in California in 1978 and spread
throughout the country, contributing, probably decisively, to the
Reagan election and to the Reagan-Kemp-Roth tax laws that followed.

As McIntyre and Tipps show, the revolt had legitimate griev-
ances that were skillfully misdirected. In California, homeowner
property taxes had increased 61 percent in the three years from
1975 to 1978, the year of Proposition 13. In the same period, taxes
on business, industrial, and agricultural property were *down* 5
percent. The revolt, however, was not against this shift of the tax
burden but against taxes in general, accompanied by vague but

strident cries of "waste" and "fraud." The upshot was an even greater shift away from business taxation.

The same thing happened on the national level. Some big-business lobbyists known as the Carlton group (because they met for breakfast at the Sheraton-Carlton in Washington) had led a loose coalition in blocking President Carter's tax-reform proposals and then in widening some loopholes. This preliminary success encouraged them to refine their strategy and led to their devastating victories in 1981. Here are some of the results, as culled from the booklet:

Item: In the years 1969–80 average hourly wages went up 6 percent in constant dollars, while top executive salaries went up 71 percent.

Item: "By 1981, one-quarter of all taxpayers had more Social Security taxes withheld from their wages than they paid in federal income taxes." Social Security taxes are, of course, regressive, and of course, this year's "reform" has increased them.

Item: The Reagan-Kemp-Roth tax cuts, coupled with the 1983 Social Security tax increase, have resulted in a tax *increase* of 22 percent for those whose income is less than $10,000 but in a tax *decrease* of 15 percent for those whose income is more than $200,000. (For those whose income is between $20,000 and $30,000, the situation is about a standoff.)

Item: The rate on capital gains is now lower than the marginal income and Social Security tax rate paid by a wage earner with a family of four who earns $20,000.

The main concern of *Inequity and Decline* is with corporation taxes and their loopholes. You're probably aware that corporations—especially the *Fortune* 500 and the *Forbes* 500—pay a smaller share of the federal taxes than they used to. Back in 1950, when Harry Truman was president, the corporate income tax produced 26.5 percent of the federal revenue; by fiscal year 1983 the figure had dropped to 5.9 percent. The fall has been steady, in response to increasing pressure from businessmen and bankers and their publicists, who have been careful to insist that they really are not greedy but are anxious to increase investment in productive enterprise, for the advantage of us all.

Even before President Reagan's ironically entitled Economic Recovery Tax Act of 1981, United States business was taxed much more lightly than that of Japan or of any Western European nation—with one exception. This fact and its exception should give pause to hard-nosed pragmatic men of affairs, accustomed to judging things by how they really work rather than by how someone who's never met a payroll says they ought to work. For the exception was Great Britain, which was also the only one of all those nations whose productivity grew less than ours in the 1970s.

And this brings us back to *The Affluent Society*. Our recent experience shows that the question of progressive vs. regressive taxation is not one that can be postponed to some more propitious time, nor can it be safely separated from other social concerns. Conservative tax policies are as destructive as conservative social policies; one leads to massive and degrading unemployment, the other to an impoverished society. When he wrote *The Affluent Society*, even when he published the third edition in 1976, Galbraith could not imagine that the conservatives would be so blind and so brutal as to throw fourteen million of their fellow citizens out of work and complacently plan to keep them there. Although sarcastic and witty at their expense, he was more generous in his opinion of them than that. He was, in fact, generous to a fault, the only fault in his great book.

[1/83]

The Last Chapter in Keynes

Among the saddest modern words of tongue or pen is the last chapter of John Maynard Keynes's *The General Theory of Employment, Interest and Money.* It was not meant to be sad. It was written in exultation by a man of fifty-two at the height of his powers. He had been editor of the *Economic Journal*, the world's most prestigious publication in his field, for twenty-five years. He was the author of several influential political pamphlets and four major books, one of them an international best-seller, another a groundbreaking two-volume *Treatise on Money.* He was active and known and listened to in Cambridge, Manchester, Whitehall, and the City of London.

As he wrote the final chapter, he could look back with satisfaction on five years of hard work on a book he was frank to say he expected would change the world. The people with whom he had discussed his ideas and to whom he had submitted proofs of the work in progress encouraged him in that expectation, though he scarcely needed encouragement. He was self-confident to the brink of arrogance. At the same time, he had a saving wit (those who felt its occasional sting were not so sure it was "saving") that was often turned toward himself. How else can we interpret the title he gave his great book? *The General Theory,* indeed! Did he rank himself with Einstein? Of course he did. Did he find it amusing that he should be so pushy? Yes, that too.

The heart of the whole work is in the last chapter's first sentence: "The outstanding faults of the economic society in which we live are its failure to provide for full employment and its arbitrary and inequitable distribution of wealth and incomes." I can only think that most economists reading that sentence have shrugged as they shrug when, let us say, a politician makes obligatory declarations in favor of school and family — two institutions everyone believes in and no one proposes to do anything substantial about. Then they probably have skimmed lightly to the famous peroration concerning "ideas, not vested interests, which are dangerous for good or evil," and have returned contentedly to the construction and deconstruction of their mathematical models.

Keynes, however, intended his ideas to be "dangerous for good." The economy's faults were "dangerous for evil" — not inconvenience, but evil. The economy would not work properly unless they were corrected. Every aspect of *The General Theory* depended upon and was directed toward that correction. Few noticed.

At a crucial point in Chapter 6 Keynes shows the fallacy of the classical theory that saving drives the economy. He writes: "Saving, in fact, is a mere residual." At the end of the chapter he announces that "the conception of the *propensity to consume* will, in what follows, take the place of the propensity or disposition to save."

Okay, say mathematically trained economists, wherever *S* appears in our equations we'll substitute *C*. But they pay no attention to the distribution of incomes. Indeed, their procedure is one of deduction from axioms, with all reference to actual situations rigorously excluded. The result is confusion.

In the modern economy of mass production, while it may not make much difference who does the saving, it makes all the difference in the world who does the consuming. Affairs might be so badly skewed that only one person did all the saving, and the system could creak along reasonably well. But the system would not work at all if one person did all the consuming (a manifest absurdity); and it will not work very well when 20 percent of the people do a mere 4.3 percent of the consuming (which is the way we try to run things in the United States today).

In a mass-production economy, consumption is a chore that cannot be delegated. A feudal economy can do everything it has to do when one-tenth of 1 percent of the people dine on paté of reindeer tongue, and 99.9 percent get along on carrot soup. A modern economy falters whenever a sizable percentage of the population is denied its output. If the output isn't fully consumed, there is no point in producing so much; and if there is no point in producing so much, there is no point in employing so many people, whereupon things start to unravel—rather, many things are not knitted up in the first place.

In talking about "arbitrary and inequitable distribution of wealth and incomes," Keynes wasn't ritualistically endorsing motherhood; he was pointing to the heart of the problem. This was so obvious that he didn't think it needed much emphasis. The solutions, too, were obvious, and a few of them had been in partial use: nearly confiscatory death duties, steeply progressive income taxes, possibly a cap on incomes. What would be necessary at a particular stage in a particular society might not be appropriate in another. One wouldn't know until one tried. It is also very likely, as he wrote in a previous chapter, that "the duty of ordering the current volume of investment [to achieve full employment] cannot safely be left in private hands." Again, one could not say in advance exactly how this should be organized.

Keynes taught himself probability theory, and wrote a fat book about it, to satisfy himself that, as regards the future, "We simply do not know." Unfortunately, some of his most skeptical critics and some of his most enthusiastic supporters undertook to supply the unavailable knowledge. The result was what several generations of bemused undergraduates have learned to call the IS-LM curve, which is supposed to show "the simultaneous determination of equilibrium values of the interest rate and the level of national income as a result of conditions in the goods and money markets." That's what *The MIT Dictionary of Modern Economics* says; don't look at me.

And don't let it fret you. It's all a game of let's-pretend. But it distracted the economics profession from Keynes's message and sent the majority off on a treasure hunt for equilibria to make graphs and journal articles of. (Physics, the source of the idea, equates equilibrium with entropy, or the end of change, a.k.a. death. But let that pass.)

Keynes, to be sure, was not above trying to peer into the future himself. The peroration of *The General Theory* may even be taken as an example. I want to shift here, though, to an essay he wrote six years earlier. It is called "Economic Possibilities for Our Grandchildren." He advanced two propositions: First, the "economic problem" would be solved in about a hundred years, provided there were no major wars and the population did not expand too much. Second, the process would depend on the steady accumulation of capital, and that would come about by means of incentives then in force. "For at least another hundred years," he wrote, "we must pretend to ourselves and to everyone that fair is foul and foul is fair; for foul is useful and fair is not. Avarice and usury and precaution must be our gods for a little while longer still. For only they can lead us out of the tunnel of economic necessity into daylight."

The man who said "In the long run we are all dead" should have known that things seldom if ever work out as envisioned. Only 62 of his prophecy's 100 years have run, and we certainly have not avoided major wars or population explosions. Nor have we seen recent signs of the sort of capital accumulation that Keynes expected to lead us into daylight. As for the interest rate, which he expected to trend steadily downward and effect "the euthanasia of the functionless investor," it is (even at today's supposedly low rates) higher than it ever was in his lifetime.

Two contemporaries, Bernard Shaw (whom he admired) and Lenin (whom he did not), had visions similar in form to his. In the preface to *Major Barbara*, Shaw wrote "that the greatest of our evils, and the worst of our crimes is poverty, and that our first duty, to which every other consideration should be sacrificed, is not to be poor." In the play proper, Cusins asks: "Excuse me: is there any place in your religion for honor, justice, truth, love, mercy, and so forth?" Undershaft replies: "Yes: they are the graces and luxuries of a rich, strong, and safe life."

Lenin, foreseeing the establishment of the Communist state, wrote in *The State and Revolution:* "Capitalist culture has created large-scale production, factories, railways, the postal service, telephones, etc., and on this basis the great majority of the functions of the old 'state power' have become so simplified and can be reduced to such exceedingly simple operations of registration, filing, and checking that they can be quite easily performed by every literate person."

These three visions all rely on a situation or change of one sort to effect a change of another. In each case, foul or death-dealing or self-serving motives are supposed to be led, one might almost say by an invisible hand, to lay the foundations of the good life.

Let us assume the foundations at last to be laid. Why should the original motives cease to be effective? Why should men and women who have succeeded with "avarice, usury, and precaution" now abdicate? Undershaft obviously enjoys his religion of being a millionaire and his control of money and gunpowder. Why give it all up for "graces and luxuries" he already has? Even in the Lenin example, where the same people may be involved first and last, one wonders why self-serving bureaucrats become dedicated and efficient public servants (for surely that was Lenin's expectation—and we have lived to see it disappointed).

More important, how can you and I and Keynes himself— understanding the difference—renounce the fair and embrace the foul? What an obscene pretense is asked of us!

Well, "Economic Possibilities for Our Grandchildren" is perhaps a playful aberration in Keynes. His steady theme elsewhere is that economics is one of the "moral sciences" (a phrase he no doubt learned from his Comtian father). His formal ethics was heavily influenced by the hedonism of G. E. Moore and thus was a far cry from that of, say, the National Conference of Catholic Bishops—as both his and theirs are from mine. Yet he and I could have agreed with the bishops when they wrote, "Every economic decision and institution must be judged in the light of whether it protects or undermines the dignity of the human person."

Keynes's initial disagreement with classical economics was that it denied the existence and even the possibility of involuntary unemployment. Today the economics profession either accepts a "natural" rate of unemployment, which may be as high as 7 or 8 percent, or rejects the relevance of ethics altogether. The high road surveyed in *The General Theory*, and described in its last chapter, was not taken.

It might have been.

[6/92]

Envoi

It is common knowledge, and freely reported by the press, that the Federal Reserve Board really wants to hurt the housing market, because it wants to hurt the construction industry, because it wants employment and wage scales constrained, because it wants to send a message that it is serious about inflation.

If you are not profoundly shocked by that sentence, please read it again. It shows the depths of savagery below which we have fallen. I say "below" because savages tend to share with their fellows in lean times; and those who seek to unload their troubles on a scapegoat usually try to choose one arguably blameworthy. Our behavior is not so civilized. In lean times we become mean, and we boast of it.

Since we are all members one of another, since what we do unto others we do to ourselves, the most important of the costs of production is labor. More people are primarily involved in labor than in any other cost, and more people are arbitrarily excluded from participating in the society to which they nominally belong.

The arbitrary exclusion is an official act of the Federal Reserve Board, an arm of the United States government, which raises the interest rate with the express intent of restricting the employment of labor and preventing increases in the wage scale. This intent has been formed and announced despite the fact that tens of millions of our fellow citizens are living lives of desperation that is not always quiet. The message they receive is that the society has small concern and less respect for them.

The members of the Federal Reserve Board who have raised the interest rate, and the economists and speculators who have applauded their action, may protest that they intended no such message. But the message certainly has been received, and it certainly is as clear as the message that the Federal Reserve Board is serious about inflation.

It is a mark of strength of the American tradition that in relation to their numbers so few of the rejected have lost trust in their compatriots and respect for themselves, developed what the late Erik Erikson described as a negative identity, and lashed out against the society that rejects them. Some of those with street smarts or suburban smarts or rural slum smarts are of course already lashing out. They impose such severe moral, emotional, and fiscal costs on society and on themselves that one must wonder whether the policy of rejection may not be as imprudent as it is unjust.

DATE DUE

The Library Store   #47-0103